Restorative Justice

Another Side of Justice

Healing & Redemption

The premise of Restorative Justice was derived from tribal cultures such as the indigenous people of America and New Zealand. Whenever anyone was harmed by another in the tribal community, the tribal members required restitution be made to the victim and the community at large. That premise is the same methodology behind today's Restorative Justice Movement.

Restorative Justice - Healing & Redemption

Copyright 2009 by Carol S. Harcarik

Registered with the Library of Congress
Copyright Office

Published by Hartington Press, LLC
N6638 Shorewood Hills Road
Lake Mills, Wisconsin 53551
Email: hartingtonpress@aol.com

Cover Design: Copyright 2009 by Carol S. Harcarik
Cover Model Copyright: Tad Denson - Information filed with Shutterstock Images LLC

Editors: John Lehman, Julie Clark
Copy Editor: Paula Pisani

Dedication

To Thomas S. Skillman, my ninety-seven year old father, who continues to inspire me every day. He taught me the love of story telling when I was a little girl. I would sit on his lap and stare in wide-eyed wonderment as he told me stories of how he often went hunting with Davy Crocket. I believed every word.

To Mary Ann Jackson, my friend, for sending me on a journey into the amazing world of Restorative Justice.

To the courageous victims and offenders I interviewed. They changed my life and my perspective on how I now live my life.

The Cure of Troy

by Seamus Heaney

Human beings suffer.
They torture one another.
The get hurt and get hard,
No poem or play or song
Can fully right a wrong
Inflicted and endured.

History says, don't hope
On this side of the grave,
But then, once in a lifetime
The longed-for tidal wave
Of justice can rise up
And hope and history rhyme.

So hope for a great sea-change
On the far side of revenge.
Believe that a farther shore
Is reachable from here.
Believe in Miracles
And cures and healing wells.

If there's fire on the mountain
And lightning and storm
And a god speaks from the sky
That means someone is hearing
The outcry and the birth-cry
Of new life at its term.

It means once in a lifetime
That justice can rise up
And hope and history rhyme.

Abridged Version

INTRODUCTION

Restorative Justice Is Changing The World

Restorative Justice is a victim-oriented, grass-roots and community-based justice system that is spreading around the world. Included are all types of crime in the criminal justice arena. Its methodology is also being used to help resolve international conflicts.

Restorative Justice focuses on the harm caused to victims. This harm has a ripple affect that extends to the victim's family, friends and members of the community. To try to heal the harm many Restorative Justice Programs offer opportunity for victims and offenders to come face to face for dialogue either through a circle of victims and offenders or individually, with the help of facilitators.

This process allows the victims the opportunity to address the harm done to them by openly discussing with the offenders the pain and agony they have suffered as a result of their crimes -- plus the victims are able to give voice to the fact that they have been left with grievous, unfulfilled needs.

Restorative Justice's goal is to help heal these needs. Hopefully, the victims leave the dialogue experience with less fear, with many unanswered questions finally put to rest and a realization that their needs have been recognized as the most important element in the process. They are also given options to help in their healing and if they choose to forgive or reconcile with their offender, it is not an expectation, it is their choice.

Restorative Justice – Healing & Redemption

Victim/offender dialogue helps to humanize the offenders and gives them an opportunity to right the wrong they've done by combining accountability with restitution and punishment. As an outcome, the offenders are often transformed and find redemption.

Victims frequently learn that their offenders were victims, too. This commonality between them can be shocking and unexpected, but it often starts a chain reaction of positive emotional responses. Some victims are also surprised when they realize the offenders are often suffering from guilt and remorse. These powerful emotional events can help to meet the victim's needs and open the door to possible reconciliation.

Restorative Justice processes are being used for criminal justice issues in numerous countries in the world and in almost all states in the U.S. They include: Victim/offender dialogue which can only be initiated by the victim; creative sentencing that make offenders accountable to their victims; mediation and many different types of programs for rehabilitation and crime prevention; and drug & alcohol courts offering treatment instead of the revolving door of jail sentences. These processes provide a continuum of programs and applications some of which fully represent restorative principles and some partially.

All Restorative Justice practices, to be truly restorative, must directly address the needs of victims. Offenders are to be held accountable when addressing all types of crime including crimes committed by juveniles, murder, rape, other sexual crimes and domestic abuse. Restorative Justice, at least in the form of dialogue, would not be appropriate for the small percentage of sociopaths and psychotic criminals but could address their accountability. For all of us this is a paradigm shift when thinking about the needs of crime victims in our communities and the harm caused to them. When seeking justice in our current adversarial justice system, the victim is left out of the process. This is counter productive and does not complete the circle of crime and punishment and offers no opportunity for healing and redemption. Restorative Justice gives opportunities for healing to the victim by addressing their needs and by offering a different philosophical approach. As an outcome, the offender is often affected in a positive way, thus, giving a balance to the end result.

Furthermore, we now have measurable data from the various Restorative Justice programs throughout the United States. We know that for juvenile offenders who go through Restorative Justice Programs, the adjudication rates are dropping and so is the recidivism rate. Hard-core criminals are showing positive results in their prison behavior after taking Restorative Justice training programs and participating in victim/offender dialogues. Plus we are seeing their recidivism rate drop. **The victim is at the heart of this positive change because their trauma is reduced and they've had help in their healing process.**

It is clear that the current system is not working and changes are needed to promote offender accountability and for victims to avoid further victimization. In addition, our prisons are dangerously overcrowded resulting in unnecessary violence and lacking in meaningful programs for inmates. As a society we need to wake up to the explosive situations in our prison population. Sentencing juveniles as adults, when we know they are not, is only one of the major issues that needs to be addressed. Adding to the enormity of the problem, we are imprisoning the poor, the less educated members of our society and dealing with rampant racial inequalities in our prisons.

According to Gary Hilton, former Assistant Commissioner in the New Jersey State Department of Corrections there are approximately two million federal and state prisoners in the United States and thirteen million who are processed in county correctional facilities in one year's time. He feels a positive action that would reduce a large portion of our prison population is to send people who are dealing with drug and alcohol addiction to rehabilitation centers. "Addiction is not criminal behavior," he strongly states.

Restorative Justice just may be the answer in the criminal justice arena, the answer to international conflict among nations of the world, and for other areas in our society, for example, in schools for bullying issues and in the work place for conflict resolution. So far the results are hopeful and promising.

In the United States, the Restorative Justice movement started in Indiana in the late 1970s. Now, almost every state in the union has some type of Restorative Justice Program. The state of Wisconsin is becoming a model for the nation by using Restorative Justice for juveniles and hard-core criminals. Minnesota's Restorative Justice programs are spreading across the state. Dr. Mark Umbreit who heads the Center for Restorative Justice and Peacemaking at the University of Minnesota and who is a founder of the movement, is leading the way.

Restorative Justice's powerful face to face dialogue process is now being used extensively in political, religious and cultural conflicts throughout the world like the Israeli/Palestinian conflict. Dr. Umbreit, along with many others, are responsible for making enormous international efforts in Restorative Justice that is now literally exploding around the world and developing in Australia, Canada, numerous European countries, Japan, New Zealand, South Africa, some South American countries and many other parts of the world. There is reason for "Hope!"

Personal note from the Author: *My journey into the intricacies of Restorative Justice has been a difficult and emotional experience but also full of enlightenment. That enlightenment has turned into a passion and a need to reveal what it really means for our society.*

I heard about Restorative Justice through a friend and neighbor, Mary Ann Jackson. After I told her I wanted to write a book on first offenders, she told me about Judge Edward R. Brunner in Barron County, Wisconsin and the amazing progress Barron County was making with juveniles by using Restorative Justice. Since I knew nothing about it, I read every book, every article and visited every website on the subject that I could find. After about six months of research, I was convinced that it could never work. However, since I had put so much effort into the subject I

Restorative Justice – Healing & Redemption

made an appointment with Judge Brunner. He had provided the vision and became the founder of the Restorative Justice Program in Barron County.

Polly Wolner, who is the Executive Director of their Program was responsible for its implementation into the community.

Polly, along with the community of Barron County have created an incredibly successful program. When I left Barron County, after spending two full days seeing what they had accomplished, I became a passionate believer in Restorative Justice. They had cut their adjudication rates for juveniles by seventy percent and began using Restorative Practices in the schools for prevention. It was working and they could prove it.

Shortly after exploring Barron County I had the unique opportunity of interviewing Professor Janine Geske at Marquette Law School in Milwaukee, Wisconsin where she teaches Restorative Justice. Her passion for Restorative Justice is absolutely infectious. Several times a year she goes to prisons and runs Restorative Justice Circles with victims and inmates. She finds this experience to be so profound and moving that it always renews her belief in Restorative Justice's power to heal.

Then I was fortunate enough to meet Dr. Mark Umbreit who heads the Center for Restorative Justice and Peacemaking at the University of Minnesota. As one the founding fathers, he is very involved in the spiritual part of this movement and believes that the healing and transformation that occurs through dialogue, between adversaries, is life changing and world changing. He has witnessed this transformation many times and travels the world with his message of hope. At his Center in Minnesota he trains people to work as facilitators in criminal justice and in the international arena to resolve regional conflicts through the use of Restorative Justice principles.

10

Restorative Justice – Healing & Redemption

I also had the pleasure of meeting Judge Alex Calabrese who directs one of the nations's first Community Justice Centers in Brooklyn, New York using Restorative Justice Practices. He is inspiring, devoted and committed to the people in his precinct, particularly, the low-income minority population in the community of Red Hook. In a few short years, Judge Calabrese and the hard-working people employed at the Red Hook Community Justice Center turned a crime-ridden crack-infested community into a prosperous and safe place. People from all over the world visit the Center trying to replicate his success in their troubled communities.

Dr. Howard Zehr, is affectionately known as the grandfather of Restorative Justice and author of numerous books on the subject. He spends many hours working with victim groups and is the Co-Director of the Graduate Center for Justice and Peacebuilding at Eastern Mennonite University in Harrisonburg, Virginia. Many of his books were included in my research and he became an advisor and mentor to me during the writing of this book. I am very grateful to him for his insights into the affect Restorative Justice has on the victim.

My book, "Restorative Justice Is Changing the World" is a result of the inspiration of these people and many others that I have interviewed. It contains true stories that graphically describe how, when done properly, Restorative Justice can make a huge difference in the lives of decent law-abiding citizens by making their communities safer while saving millions for the taxpayer. Restorative Justice's application in international conflict, is also reflected in this book, through its use in the Israeli/Palestinian conflict and in the criminal justice system of New Zealand.

My hope is that this book will inspire you, my reader, to participate in Restorative Justice in your community. There really is reason to hope for a better world!

Table of Contents

Section I - Restorative Justice True Stories

Section II - Restorative Justice International

Section III - Violentization

Section IV - Restorative Justice Models

Section I

Restorative Justice

Criminal Justice Stories

Restorative Justice – Healing & Redemption

In the following true stories about
Criminal Justice
some names and locations have been
changed to protect the privacy of
certain individuals.

Kathy – Victim of Serial Rapist Todd – Rapist

Restorative Justice Victim/Offender Dialogue

*Rape damages the soul as well as the body.
It is an act of degradation and violence
that does irreparable harm.*

Kathy's Story of Rape

At fifteen years old, Kathy was a cute, spunky teenager with a bubbling personality. She had led a sheltered and protected life since she was the youngest of six siblings, lived in a small Midwestern town and attended a private school at the local Baptist Church where her father was the pastor. There were only about seven other students in her class.

That summer, she met Todd at a local campground where her family was spending the weekend and he flirted with her constantly. She was delighted and relished all the attention. "I was completely smitten by him," she said. "He was so good looking, and I was just a skinny little small-town girl." She had never given a boy her phone number, but before she left the campground that day with her family, she tentatively left a note addressed to Todd in the campground office. That very evening he called her. He told her that he was seventeen, lived in a small town near her home and was on his high school's football and wrestling teams. During their phone conversation he made a point to tell her, "You'll hear a lot of things about me that are not true. I just want to be totally honest with you and tell you that I do have a juvenile record but its all a lie. Don't believe anything you hear about me." Kathy paid little attention to this information and considered herself very fortunate that Todd appeared to be interested in her. To Kathy, he appeared to be a real jock and she was overwhelmed with excitement when he asked her for a date. She added that at the same time she remembers also feeling somewhat confused by his attention and interest in her. "Why me," she thought. They began dating and were together almost every day of the week that summer.

Kathy's parents found Todd to be a charming, nice young man and he quickly won their trust. However, after he and Kathy had been dating for about two and half months their relationship became more and more turbulent. They seemed to be dealing with many different issues; the most troubling one was that Todd was very sexually aggressive. He kept insisting on having sex with her and she kept insisting she had been taught not to have sex until she was married and that she planned on keeping it that way.

So, after two and half months of a stormy relationship with Kathy constantly refusing his advances, Todd decided he was not going to listen to her excuses anymore. It was near the end of summer and they were planning on spending the evening at his home eating pizza and watching some movies. His mother was upstairs sleeping when they arrived. Only shortly into the first movie, Todd started coming on to Kathy just like he had in the past. She tried to make light of the situation by being giggly and pushing him away saying "Hey, come on, we're watching a movie."

Normally when he exhibited this aggressive behavior, she would reject his advances and then he would pout for awhile and get over it. She just expected his usual response. But this night there wouldn't be any moping for him. He grabbed her, would not take no for an answer, pushed her down on the floor on her back, took her arms and held them tightly over her head, used a wrestling hold on her legs with his knees, pulled down her pants and underwear with his other hand and then proceeded to brutally rape her as she kept begging, **"No, No, Please Stop,"**

Kathy said with bitterness in her voice, "I was so stunned that he wouldn't stop and kept thinking, 'This can't be happening' and I didn't know what to do. I was afraid to scream because I was familiar with his temper and frightened that he would hurt me. Also, If I did scream, his mom would have come down and he would have been in big trouble and who knows what he would have done to me then. He did not use any weapons to scare me but his mere size was enough intimidation. I weighed a mere ninety pounds and was about five foot eight inches tall compared to his six foot and one-hundred-and-seventy-pound body. He lifted weights regularly and was substantially bigger and stronger than me. I did not have a chance to fight him off." She added, "To make the situation even worse Todd did not use any protection."

"After he finished, he laid down on top of me while I was crying and whispered, 'I love you' in my ear -- that statement was to really mess me up for a very long time. Then he just laid there breathing into my ear for what seemed like forever."

Finally he said, "You are going to be a mess you better go to the bathroom and clean up."

Eager to get away from him, Kathy quickly ran into the bathroom, cleaned up and then started thinking about what she should do next. Her mind was racing. At about that moment, she recalled, "It seemed like a switch went off in my head, and I began to say to myself, 'I have been a horrible girlfriend by making Todd wait for sex and now look what he did. Good girl friends don't make their boy friends wait. This is all my fault.'"

Then she was forced to face the fact that she wasn't a virgin anymore and what was she going to do about that. She had no preparation from her parents on how to behave after an experience like this. Her mind was exploding and she kept repeating to herself, "What am I going to do?" In her family you stayed a virgin until you were married. Suddenly, the answer popped into her mind. She knew exactly what she would have to do and that was to marry Todd. Nothing else mattered. Kathy believed this to be her only option because she was taught that you only have sex with the person you are going to marry.

Of course, at this point, Todd was ready to dump her and go on to the next victim.

(This twisted type of reaction from Kathy is typical of many rape-crisis victims. They quickly blame themselves because they don't fully understand what really happened to them.)

Kathy Ignored Warning Signs

The next day, when Kathy calmed down a bit, she began to piece together all the warning signs she had ignored. "When I first starting dating Todd I didn't really know anyone from his circle of friends because he went to a different high school than I did, but it often seemed that he was popular and had a lot of friends around him. As time went on though, strangely, there seemed to be an equal number of people who liked him and people who hated him. There were girls who wanted to date him and girls who screamed hateful remarks at him. There were guys who seemed to really like him and an equal number who wanted to beat him up. He told me that he had been kicked out of high school because of all the incidents that he said were lies and he was going to a smaller private school."

According to Kathy, they started dating Memorial Day weekend and were together constantly that summer. After the first couple of weeks, she said, "I was under constant pressure for sex. He was often, also, mean to me in public and exhibited odd behavior. Like one day when we went to a waterpark -- he made fun of my body all day long saying my breasts weren't big enough and that I looked like a little kid." He would say, "I've seen twelve-year olds with bigger breasts than you have."

He talked to her like that all day long and then disappeared for an hour or two while she walked around by herself. Then he found her and said, "Where were you?"

20

Kathy added, "Todd was also a skilled manipulator because I observed how he charmed my parents. In the beginning of our relationship, he spent as much time with them as possible. My parents were a bit overprotective because my six brothers and sisters had all graduated and I was the caboose, the only one left at home. Todd put that situation together quickly and was always sucking up to them. It worked, because they appeared to like him. Consequently, they would let me go out with him and go anywhere I wanted because they trusted him."

The other difficult characteristic Todd had was how controlling he was. When Kathy told him that her friends did not like him and thought she should stop dating him, he screamed angrily, "If you are going to date me you cannot see any of your friends." Kathy said, "Of course, my friends were already alienated towards me because they did not like Todd, but for some reason I did not resist his commands. I guess I was still in shock that this cute guy wanted to date me. This all seems obscene to me, after the fact, but I was really dumb-founded that he was interested in me. I guess it must have been a self-esteem issue with me, " she said.

Kathy described three incidents that occurred during her relationship with Todd and they clearly define a young man who is out of control but, unfortunately, that was not evident to a star-struck naive teenager.

The first incident occurred in the first few weeks of dating and followed one of the many times Kathy refused Todd's sexual advances. He was very angry and was driving her home. When they arrived he shouted at her to get out of the car and she shouted back, "No, I want to talk to you about it." Then he started screaming at the top of his lungs, "Just get out of the car." He reached over her and tried to open the car door on her side and she tried to pull it shut but in the process his thumb was jammed in the door. Then he just flipped out. He forcibly pushed her aside, opened the car door and shoved her out. Fortunately, she was unhurt. Her response to the incident was self-deprecating, "I was dumb enough to keep dating him after that, because he apologized. He said he would control his anger and be more respectful to me."

The second incident also dealt with a sexual issue. From the beginning of their relationship Kathy had taken a strong stand that she would not have sex until she was married. A perfect example of Todd not accepting this ultimatum was a weekend in mid-June when she and Todd spent a weekend at her brother's home. Her brother ran a youth ministry at his church and he would often have huge numbers of kids for weekend retreats. Kathy had attended these retreats in the past and had many fun-filled memories and had met great kids; but on this summer weekend, Todd, had come along with her. After a great day, some of the kids went home but many stayed for the night sleeping in the recreation room on the floors and couches. During the night Kathy woke up twice in the middle of the night and each time she found Todd on top of her, ready for sex, trying to get her pants down. Each time she pushed him off and expressed her anger with his behavior.

"Because there were so many kids there he had to 'stuff it' and not show his rage and frustration. I was absolutely mortified and worried that somebody might have seen what he was doing and think it was OK with me and tell my brother. I was pretty upset with him again," she said.

The third incident happened on the fourth of July weekend. They had gone to a huge riverfest fireworks celebration and spent some time walking around the grounds. They ran into some girls who started screaming hateful comments at Todd and at the same time trying to warn Kathy that he was going to have sex with her and dump her. They were very persistent with their warnings and kept cursing at Todd. They also ran into guys threatening to beat him up. Kathy said she was dazed and confused by all this.

As they walked to the area set aside for watching fireworks, Todd blurted out, "Well I'm going and I will meet you back here at ten o'clock for the fireworks." Kathy quickly responded, "You are going to do what, you can't just leave me here alone." He replied, "Well, I've got to." So he just left her standing there. It was eight o'clock and Kathy found herself frightened and alone surrounded by a lot of drunk people. She knew her parents would have killed her if they knew she had gotten herself into this kind of situation. (She later discovered the reason he left her there alone was because he was raping another girl.)

Feeling rather dismal and scared she found herself walking aimlessly around in the dark, but luckily, after only a short time she stumbled into an ex-boyfriend of hers. He wanted to know why she was there all by herself. "My boyfriend just left me here," she said. So, he invited her to hang out with him and his buddies. Later, shortly before the fireworks were to begin, Kathy was walking around with these guys and they ran into Todd. He went berserk when he saw her with a group of guys and, while everyone was looking, he got in her friend's face and started swearing and punching him. Kathy's friend had just been trying to protect her so he started to fight back and yelled at Todd, "What kind of guy are you leaving Kathy here all alone?" At this point, all of Todd's friends appeared and they were ready to start a major confrontation. Kathy said, "Here I was standing in the middle of this mess. I asked my friend to just leave with his buddies because the odds did not look good and I did not want to be responsible for someone getting hurt." Fortunately, her friends quickly disappeared and a crisis was averted.

As soon as they were out of sight, Todd said to her, "I am not watching the fireworks with you." He left her standing there alone again, it was completely dark and time for the fireworks to start. She walked away crying and ran into the same friends. They gave her a hug and moved back into a spot where they could not be seen and watched the fireworks together. After the show, she thanked them, said goodbye and went to find Todd so he could take her home. She waited and waited and he finally showed up and told her that she should not have made him mad. For Kathy, the whole evening had been so crazy and she was super embarrassed and very disappointed in Todd.

Kathy attempts to End the Relationship

After these three incidents, Kathy had enough. She called Todd and told him she was breaking up with him and went away for a week with her brother and his girlfriend. When she returned there was a letter in the mail from Todd. He said he was sorry that he had treated her so badly and said it wouldn't happen again and that he needed to control his anger.

She didn't respond to his letter or return any of his phone calls for about two weeks but he was very persistent and she finally broke down and started talking to him again. He seemed remorseful and appeared to have actually changed and convinced her to come out to a family barbecue.

Kathy justified the reason she went back to him after all these bad experiences by saying, "He did seem really sorry for his behavior and was very convincing that he was going to change. I guess you could say he was an exceptionally good liar because I actually believed him."

One of the things that always surprised Kathy about Todd was that during the entire time they were dating, she never saw any evidence of Todd using drugs or alcohol. Maybe, because he knew about her family's strong religious values, he would not have drank in front of her anyway.

At the barbecue, Todd offered her a diamond ring, giving her three to choose from. He said the ring was proof that he had changed. Kathy reticently asked him, "Where did you get all these rings from?" He told her one was from his brother-in-law who decided not to propose and one was new and he couldn't remember where he got the third one.

He looked very serious when he said to her, "This is a promise ring." She responded, "Just because you are promising to marry me does not mean that you are going to get sex." And after making that clarative statement she choose a ring and he promised again, "I will not have sex with you until we are married and I want you to have this right now to show you how I have changed."

Kathy acknowledged, "I was stupid, young and naive enough to believe him because the next time I had a date with him was when he raped me.

Kathy decides, the Solution is Marriage

Following the rape, Todd drove her home in dead silence. The next day he called and broke up with her and wanted his ring back. Kathy refused to return the ring and kept it hostage so he could not give it to someone else.

She never told anyone in her family about the rape only that they had broken up. Somehow she managed to compartmentalize the rape in her head telling herself it really didn't matter because she was going to marry him.

Kathy also told herself, "No one can ever find out about this because someday he will be my husband."

The rape had occurred in early August and she spent the rest of August going to Todd's football scrimmages. Once, when he got hurt she even went down to the field to assist him and rode in the ambulance with him to the hospital and stayed at his side to support him.

Kathy actually convinced her parents into letting her change schools so she could go to the same school as he did. They allowed it, of course, because they had no knowledge of the rape.

"My soul's mission was clear," she reiterated. "I needed to marry Todd and I continued to be very concerned about what would happen to me if I didn't marry the person who had sex with me. I was not a virgin anymore and just assumed that all my siblings didn't have sex before their marriages. I just did not know the proper response to this kind of behavior." Kathy said sex was never a topic of conversation in her home. Apparently her parents thought she was getting sex education in school, but she wasn't. She really only had one lesson about sex. No sex until marriage, that was it. Consequently, she had little information to base a decision on.

"**Now** I realize that this was the most messed up possible thinking on the face of the Earth. To most people it makes no sense but it was the immediate response to that switch that went off in my head. My only option, regardless of the horrible things that he had done, was to marry him, Kathy said.

After Todd recovered from his football injury, he made some overtures to Kathy about continuing their relationship but changed his mind and abruptly ended it.

At this point, Kathy was going to the same school as Todd and she was able to observe him date successive girls, one after the other. She quickly realized what he was doing to those girls. The roles switched and she became the girl who was warning others, but they weren't listening.

Then one day, one of the girls he was dating came to school wearing one of Todd's other rings. She said, "I just flipped out and told her she was making a big mistake and made it clear to her what Todd had done to me," she said. When this girl told Todd what Kathy had said, he grabbed Kathy at school the next day and backed her roughly into the wall and yelled in her ear, "Bitch give me my ring back." She said, "Why? Do you have another girl you want to give it to because you used up the other two? Kathy, finally clearly, saw the pattern he was weaving and knew he was doing the same thing to multiple girls as he had done to her. She realized how fortunate she was that she had not become pregnant.

Todd is Arrested and Charged With Rape

In January, a girl from Minnesota went to the police and told them Todd had raped her. The police went to his school, where he was arrested and taken to jail. Kathy chose not to get involved and said nothing. However, the word was out around the school that she had dated him and that it had not ended well. Also, many students knew she had tried to convince other girls not to date him. The detectives came to the school and spent two days talking to witnesses and other girls who had agreed to come forward. Kathy said she was hiding in the girls restroom when the police were there but they eventually found her and she was questioned. "I faced a huge decision: Do I lie or do I tell the truth," she said.

The dilemma she found herself in helped to jog Kathy's memory. In a recent conversation with Janie, a friend of her brother's, she had confided about being raped. So, when asked by the police to testify against Todd, Kathy called Janie to ask for advice. Janie assured her she would be strong enough to handle the situation and needed to tell the truth. So, reluctantly, Kathy told police everything that had happened. Eventually, Kathy and eleven other girls came forward to testify against Todd, who was charged with twenty-two counts of rape.

Although she was not required to participate, Kathy attended the hearings leading up to Todd's trial. She was scheduled to testify only at the actual trial. At these hearings, she was accompanied by three or four male friends who came to support her. They were big strong guy friends who played football against Todd. One of those friends described the trial as creepy because Todd kept looking at him in a threatening manner, smiling slyly and then turning back and looking at him again. "It was chilling because Todd had a way of instilling fear in you," he said. The day of the trial, all the girls who were to testify were informed by the police that they had confiscated a letter that Todd had sent to a friend. In that letter he savagely touted, "I intend to kill all those bitches that got me into this. When I get out they will all be dead." Kathy said, "The letter was put in his file and I saw it and believed what he said. I was sure when he got out he would try to kill me. I am not hard to miss because my family lives and owns a local business in the area where the rape occurred."

Kathy had never told her parents anything about the rape but the day of the trial her mother and father tearfully gave her a ruby ring as a gift. Her parents knew where she was going because they had signed a release from school. They were standing outside their home hugging her and telling her they loved her. As she hesitantly said good-bye, her dad told her he was coming with her and Kathy said, "No, I don't want you to come and if you do I'll have you removed." She left knowing her father was very upset, went on to the trial and was ushered into a room containing all the other girls scheduled to testify. As she entered the room, she saw her father and told the bailiffs present that if he stayed she would not testify. He was gently escorted out of the courtroom and waited outside for her.

"I am sure my parents were in a great deal of pain. I knew they felt guilty because they let me go places with Todd and because they actually liked and trusted him," Kathy said. "If my daughter had been raped, I would have felt responsible. Their approach was not to push me to talk about it and they believed when I was ready I would share with them what I could. I knew they loved me."

Todd managed to turn everything around by accepting a plea deal. By pleading guilty to eleven counts of rape he got sixteen years in prison with eligibility for parole in five. The charge was forcible rape not assault. "It was strange being in a courtroom hearing Todd being sentenced to sixteen years in prison because I had just turned sixteen and that seemed like a lifetime to me," Kathy said. Since I was so young, I did not understand the legal system and it did not occur to me what 'parole in five' meant, but I was to later find out."

All the girls who were ready to testify were young and naive when they were raped and none of them fully understood the consequences of what had happened to them and the judicial procedures they had just witnessed. They were all equally terrified to testify against Todd. When told they did not have to testify, their relief was so great they starting cheering and celebrating. However, the good mood did not last long. The atmosphere turned grave when they went back into the courtroom and heard Todd plead guilty, watched him being sentenced and sent off to jail.

Kathy deals with the aftermath of Rape

Now that Todd was safely out of the way Kathy went back to her life -- a life that would never be the same. The ramifications of living with being raped were only beginning to manifest in her mind. These manifestations would change her life and almost destroy it.

She ended up just hating school. So she attended night school, summer school and then returned to the Christian school she had previously attended and graduated from high school a year early. She was the only person in her graduating class. She felt friendless, fearful and isolated but did not realize it was because of the rape.

She also had begun dating one of the guys who had accompanied her to the trial. He was a year older than her and she readily admitted, "The real reason I was dating him was because he was big and strong and could protect me. I knew Todd was in prison but that death threat he made against me was always in the back of my mind."

Along with everything else, her attitude about sex had changed dramatically. "I never wanted to be raped again so I just gave in to sex," she said. At age eighteen, while attending college she discovered she was pregnant. Her twin girls were born in October and the following April she became engaged to her strong protector.

During premarital counseling the local pastor asked Kathy and her husband-to-be why they were rushing into marriage because they were very young and they seemed to have worked things through, even with two babies. Kathy stated, "I just got a parole notice for Todd and I need to get married because I need protection. Todd is planning to kill me." Strangely, neither the pastor nor her future husband responded to Kathy's motivation for marriage.

She was married in November, her twin girls were about fifteen months old, she was nineteen and her husband was twenty. It turned out to be almost impossible to have a normal marriage because of the unresolved issues surrounding the rape. For example Todd had said, "I love you" after he raped her. Every time Kathy's husband said that, she just cringed. The most paramount unresolved issue, however, was the fear she had of Todd and it governed her every move.

The parole notice had triggered the reality that Todd was going to eventually get out of prison. He had threatened to kill her and now she had two children to protect. This fear would slowly intensify and become an integral part of her life and was always in the background of practically all the decisions she made. She felt like a sitting duck because she was the easiest target of all the girls he raped. She still lived near the same town where the rape had occurred and her family had a business there. Todd would have no trouble finding her and carrying out his threat.

So she began to build a strategy to always have protection around her and her children. To her, that seemed like a practical decision and a path to survival. "I had to always have someone to protect me. I could not be alone and I did not ever want to be raped again," she said. "Of course, this was no way to begin a new marriage which was certainly rocky from the start because it was based on all the wrong motivations." These unresolved issues would lead to four separations plus multiple affairs for Kathy. "My rationale for the affairs was that if my husband left me, I wanted to make sure I had a backup ready to step in to protect me and my children," she said.

At the same time, her husband had some issues of his own. He never truly believed Kathy was raped, so he dealt with that by making unflattering comments about her. Like telling her she was overweight when she was practically anorexic weighing about one hundred and nineteen pounds. This, of course only added to their problems.

"When I had an affair, eventually, I would leave and we would separate for awhile," she said

"This pattern continued as I followed the news of Todd's parole hearings and then eventually learned he would soon be released from prison after serving about eleven years of his sentence. The sixteen-year prison sentence did not turn out to be a lifetime."

"From the time I received notice of Todd soon release from prison that's when the really intense fear developed," she said.

Kathy said, "The threatening letter Todd had written before he was sentenced had freaked me out and was always in the back of my mind. Knowing that he was going to get out of prison was terrifying. I was so afraid for my children and myself. In my mind I was one of the bitches he was coming after when he got out. She continued, "In other words, he was going to hurt me and my family. I would often imagine being at the mall with my four little children (my husband and I had two more children by that time) and coming face to face with him and just falling apart leaving my children unprotected. I was truly immobilized by fear, often having panic attacks because over the years of Todd's imprisonment the fear just continued to build up. My life was just torn to shreds. Consequently, I was always afraid to go to the mall and always afraid when walking to my parked car."

Kathy & Todd come Face to Face

During the time her fear was intensifying, Kathy had a number of affairs and separations from her husband and eventually filed for divorce.

At this point, she said they did go to a marriage counselor, whose name was Gail, and she immediately zeroed in on our problem. The rape, naturally, plus the fact that I had never dealt with it individually and we had not dealt with it as a couple.

"It was destroying us. I was consumed by fear. Fortunately for me, our counselor knew about Restorative Justice, and had heard of victim/offender dialogues and suggested that would be something I should try. She felt it would be a possible way of disposing of the fear I was carrying around with me".

Following her counselor's suggestion and desperate to get control of her life Kathy called Pete DeWind, head of the Restorative Justice Program at the University of Wisconsin's School of Law in Madison, Wisconsin. She asked Pete's help in setting up a victim/offender dialogue with Todd. He contacted Todd's social worker, Rosemary, who was able to get him to agree to the dialogue. Then Pete and Rosemary began preparing him for the dialogue.

Kathy worked with Gail on her dialogue preparation for hours every week for five months. Her counselor went through everything that happened to her over and over again. Then she had Kathy verbalize what she wanted to accomplish and what her goals were.

"I was hoping for two outcomes. First, I needed to know if Todd was still intent on killing me. This was the main purpose for doing the dialogue in the first place and I really needed to know the answer to that question. Second, I felt strongly that I did not want Todd to know how badly he had affected my life. I didn't want to give him the satisfaction of knowing that at the age of twenty-six he had ruined ten years of my life. My life was a mess." During the preparations for the dialogue Kathy's divorce was still pending and she was in a waiting period to make her final decision on whether to end her marriage.

Todd went through a lot of preparation and worked hard with his social worker and Pete to get ready to come face to face with Kathy. He needed to clarify what he wanted to accomplish for himself as well as for Kathy. They also kept Kathy informed of his progress.

The face to face dialogue took place in prison in mid-July. Gail went with Kathy as her support person, Todd was there with his social worker, Rosemary and Pete attended with one of his students as an observer. Also present, was the head of the sex-offender program at the prison and a prison guard. The dialogue lasted for approximately three hours with two breaks.

Both of them sat facing each other. Kathy with her fists clenched, was very agitated and crying constantly. Todd seemed extremely uncomfortable, anxious and scared. Kathy was shocked that Todd no longer looked like the confident handsome jock she remembered but instead seemed very uptight, worn out, tired, and very tense. He did not make any eye contact with her for about the first hour. During that time he sat with his hands folded and his head bowed.

Kathy asked him a lot of pointed questions because she had heard he had been kicked out of the sex offender program and she wanted to know why. She also asked him, "What things did you work on in preparation for this dialogue? What have you learned and why did you do this to me and how do I know that it will not happen again and not happen to another person?" Kathy reiterated, "I asked him everything I could possibly think of."

Todd tried hard to answer her questions and to assure Kathy that he had been through intensive treatment. He had been removed from the sexual offender program initially; but rejoined it and finished the twenty-four-seven intensive sexual-rehabiliation program that took three years to complete. He now knew why he had raped and that he had no intention of allowing it to happen again. He knew how badly he had hurt her and did not want to hurt anyone ever again and he tried to reassure her that he would not hurt her or her family; he would not re-offend.

As Todd responded to her questions, the most profound thing Kathy learned was that he actually had a modus operandi or what is also known as a profile. She matched his profile perfectly. All of his victims were innocent young girls between fifteen and seventeen years of age with loving families. He would manipulate the girl's family to get them to trust him. It was all premeditated. He told Kathy that he actually had regular girlfriends his own age but his victims had to be young, naive and vulnerable; but also, they need-ed to be strong-willed because it made him feel powerful to take that will away from them. He said to Kathy, "You were a perfect fit for my M.O." This information was a relief to Kathy. It was not her it was her profile and there was nothing she could have done to prevent the rape. He had the whole scenario planned. She no longer felt so alone knowing there were others, like her, with the same profile. She did not feel that she got answers to all her questions, but the answers were not as important as being able to ask him the questions. That made her feel more in control.

Todd explained to Kathy, "I listened to many victim-impact panels at prison and those experiences made me realize how much harm my behavior caused my victims; but actually meeting with you face to face and realizing -- in person -- the pain I've caused you, has had a much greater impact on me. It has been transforming and once again I repeat, I do not want to create any more victims."

After he said that to her, Kathy said, she could feel some of the fear begin to release. She described the feeling, "I could actually, physically, feel the fear starting to melt away."

"I was so shocked that he was in a room with a video camera rolling and that he actually told the truth. He said in front of everyone in the room that he raped me and how he raped me. He remembered every little detail. I was so relieved that he finally told the truth and had total recall about the rape because so much time had elapsed since it happened. The rape was truly not something I had imagined, but it really happened. I finally felt validated."

About this time in the dialogue Kathy's voice got stronger, she was not crying any longer and sitting up straighter. Todd appeared to be sinking down further in his chair and his head was dropping lower.

Kathy said, "I was not planning to tell him what he had done to my life, but I felt myself getting stronger and I started to change and it was very noticeable when I watched the tape of the dialogue later. I sat forward towards him and appeared physically stronger and my fear seemed to have dissipated. I appeared different, 'Embolden.'"

Kathy told him that she was twenty-six years old with four kids and her life was a complete mess because of what he did to her. She was in the middle of getting a divorce because she always had to have a backup man in her life so that she would not be alone and have protection for her and her family. "I'm terrified to be alone, have lost all my friends and live my life in constant fear," she said.

Todd tearfully apologized and told Kathy how sorry he was. "He appeared genuine to me," she said. "At this point, I forgave him because I had to do that for myself. All of this was just eating me alive and by forgiving him I hoped to get rid of this nightmare." The dialogue turned out to be the end of the anguish for Kathy. She was now completely validated and knew for sure all this had not been imagined by her, but had happened the way she remembered it and a whole room of people had heard the truth.

Kathy finds Healing

"Not testifying at sixteen was a good thing but by the same token no one publicly heard what happened to me and I never received any determination of the truth. That festered inside of me and just tore me apart," Kathy said. "Todd was guilty but guilty to what? Even my parents did not know guilty to what. I was the only one besides him who knew what happened. It was so important to receive this validation. This had to happen for me to begin to recover. Most of the fear left me."

The dialogue was in August. After it was completed, Kathy left her husband, took her four children and moved up north. She got a job and was alone. Most of the reason for finally deciding to go ahead with the divorce was how her husband had treated her, which was just awful, she said. Their marriage lasted as long as it did not necessarily because she loved him, but because she needed his protection. Now that the fear had abated she did not need him. So she left. She was now a completely different person and needed to get to know who that person was.

"The reason for my husband's constant negative reactions to me suddenly became clear, Kathy explained. He never totally believed my story of the rape. I had starting dating him when the trial began. From the very beginning of our relationship he didn't believe me because he had been a co-wrestler with Todd and was on his wrestling team for a year. After the trial, he never said I lied but never made me feel very confident that he believed me. At some point, he told me that he thought I was telling most of the truth but that maybe it had all gone down slightly differently. So all during our marriage there was an undercurrent of anger, **from him and within me**, because he never really believed my story of the rape. Plus he had other issues from his childhood that he had never dealt with."

Kathy had come face to face with her fears and experienced a release from them, thus, giving her the emotional healing she needed. She now felt strong enough to distance herself from her husband and protector and was making an effort to try to find out who she really was. Her time away from her husband was necessary; she needed her own space for awhile. Perhaps now she would be able to work on her marriage which would have been impossible before the dialogue.

Epilogue

"After the dialogue" Kathy said, "It was very clear to me that my rape had been totally premeditated and calculated right down to the exact time it occurred. I fell into the plot Todd created -- along with a number of other young girls just like me. I was no longer afraid that he was going to come and kill me and I believed everything he said at the dialogue. He was convincing and genuine. So, consequently, most of the fear was gone. **It was an incredible healing event in my life.**

"However, I have accepted that it will probably never totally go away. The first time I ran into Todd in the grocery store, for example, my heart stopped beating and my breathing stopped for a few seconds. Fortunately, I did not have my children with me. I shoved my grocery cart to the side and left as fast as I could."

Kathy acknowledges that she does continue to talk to Todd's parole officer at least twice a year and keeps updated on his whereabouts. She said, "I just feel more comfortable knowing what his current situation is."

"Rape is something you never get over, but I did put my life back together by getting back with my husband and we managed to work out a lot of our problems. We have six children together now and were always best friends so the hard work of resolving our marital problems was certainly worth it.

She sighed as she said, "I still live near the town where Todd and his family live and I run into the family frequently and find that difficult. The grocery store I frequent is in the town where the rape occurred and other reminders are always around. Not a day goes by that I don't think about it."

"Gail, my marriage counselor, was my guardian angel because she was the person who suggested I try Restorative Justice's victim/offender dialogue. I am so grateful to have discovered its existence because it gave me the opportunity to work out all the issues that were literally destroying my life. Many victims don't even understand that this is an option for them and I don't want to even think where I would be today without Restorative Justice. **It gave me my life back.**"

Todd's Story
Serial Rapist

Todd's story is an overwhelming one. He was raped too, by his father, at the age of five. This type of sexual abuse continued until he completed eighth grade. When asked how often his father had sodomized him he said, "When I was young it seemed like it was all the time. I did not have the conceptual ability to remember the length of time between the incidents of abuse. Also, for some strange reason, the sexual abuse was connected to a memory of the color white and a feeling of being surrounded by whiteness." This recurring memory haunted him, but during his imprisonment he discovered the source. His mom sent him some pictures of the farm where he had lived when he was young and when he saw the pictures of his bedroom he noticed that the walls were white. "Suddenly, it became clear to me what the white represented, it was the walls. When my father was assaulting me I would always cry and focus on the walls and it was like I went inside the walls per se--for protection."

"My father not only abused *me* sexually but also my two brothers. He was a barbaric alcoholic and he mentally, physically and emotionally abused our entire family including my two sisters and mother." Todd bitterly expressed, "I remember getting beat with sticks in our yard, in front of my friends, because I mowed the grass wrong. He

46

also beat my mom and one time he loaded a gun and was going to shoot all of us. I clearly remember watching him in his office while he put shells in the gun. Fortunately, my uncle was present and tried to get him to stop. I actually heard my father tell my uncle, 'Get lost, I'm going to blow all their fuckin heads off.' Luckily he passed out after he loaded the gun and at that point my uncle got us all out of the house."

Todd said he was pretty young at the time this happened but concluded afterwards that it didn't really matter what my father did -- my mom was never going to leave him. She would always say, "He won't do it again." Often, when things got real bad with my father my mom would tell my brothers, sisters and me to pack up all our stuff because we were getting out of there. We would do that, expecting to actually leave the house, because we were all scared to death, and then the next morning it would be like nothing ever happened. Todd said he carried around a lot of resentment towards her for that.

"My mother, also, would often take my sisters shopping with her and leave me home alone with my father. I would beg and beg for her to take me with them. Sometimes I would run outside and hide in the ditch by the road and cry and cry as she pulled away," Todd recalled. "It felt like my mom was protecting my sisters but not protecting me. I became very angry and resentful toward my sisters and this eventually resulted in resentment toward females in general."

In seventh grade Todd had another sexual encounter that would exacerbate his already seriously distorted sexual perspective. He was assaulted by another male, one of his peers. One evening all of his wrestling buddies were staying at his family's home for the night and going together to a tournament the following day. They all went to sleep and Todd was awakened by one of his friends attempting to have oral sex with him. To Todd's amazement, he had an erection, and that convinced him that there must have been something wrong with him because he reacted this way to another male. He was terrified that he was a homosexual. He carried that thought around in his mind for years, not realizing that it was a normal physical reaction. However, that sexual encounter with his fellow wrestler just complicated his already confused view of his sexuality.

Obviously, Todd's childhood and adolescent years had been traumatic. He acknowledged, "At the beginning of my freshman year at high school, and because of my father's continued violence, I attempted a fake suicide to escape my father and to get out of the house. I sat on the railroad tracks and refused to move and was taken to a psych-unit at a local hospital where I told the doctors and nurses of my alcoholic father's physical and mental abuse. I told them how my father was always hitting all of my family with sticks. However, I did not tell the doctors about the sexual abuse -- I was too embarrassed and ashamed to do that." The doctors called his father and told him he had to quit drinking and his father said, "I have been drinking for forty-five years and I am not quittin for my fuckin son." Todd said, "Those were his exact words and I'll never forget them."

The authorities told his mom that she had to move out or they were going to put Todd in a foster home. This forced her to finally leave her husband and remove her children from this destructive environment. As a consequence, Todd's mom had five children to support and she quickly got into a difficult financial situation. She would constantly complain that she had little income to live on and this left Todd feeling responsible and guilty. At this point, however, it helped that his sisters were older, able to care for themselves and his father had not sexually abused them. But he had sexually abused his brothers. "I never asked my brothers about the abuse they received but we all knew it had happened," he said. "Today, my brothers are unbelievable, you would not want to meet them -- they are in their forties, very high-strung alcoholics, just like my father and have raging tempers." Todd added, "I am not an alcoholic and I don't have a raging temper but I did, for many years, carry around a lot of anger toward my parents."

Todd becomes a Serial Rapist

Todd held his head in his hands and moaned in anguish as he said, "I never wanted to be like my father but in the end, it turned out, that I really was just like my father. In a sense, worse than my father. At the time I raped, no one would have been able to convince me that I was like him but I believe it now."

"Toward the latter part of my freshman year in high school, my parents were divorced and my father was finally not around to abuse me -- I started acting out and began a raping spree which lasted for two or three years. In my head I was raping girls to prove that I was not a homosexual plus I needed to always be in control and was full of unresolved anger. The more girls I went to bed with the more I felt like a man and I needed to prove that to myself. If a girl rejected me, I would interpret that to mean they suspected I was gay, so that made me even more persistent. I honestly believed the girls I raped would eventually, want me, and like it and sometimes that actually happened. If anyone cried when I was in the middle of a rape, I was compelled to stop. Because if I did not stop, I would be just like my father and I did not want to be like my father. So, I told myself that I was not as bad as him, because I always made sure I stopped if a girl cried."

Todd's modus operandi or MO contained some specific characteristics that he required in his victims. They needed to be young, vulnerable, in his peer group and also feisty because he wanted to overpower them. He knew all his victims and wanted them to believe they were in a dating relationship with him. That made it OK in his mind and justified his behavior. Also, he needed the trust of their parents so he managed to charm them with the image he created by combining his athletic jock-like appearance and smooth charming style. "Most of the time I was successful." he said. "Frankly, I had done such a good job that a lot of girls felt no one would believe them if they told on me. I know that sounds egotistical, but it was true."

"Girls did warn their friends not to date me because I had developed a rather bad reputation. I went from one girl to another and never wanted the current victim to hear bad stuff about me from other girls. I guess you could say I tried to control the information my victims got from their friends. But, essentially, I think I was angry that they were talking about me in a negative way. I did not want to hear what they were saying about me."

Some of his rapes actually occurred right in front of his friends. Todd said that just gave me more reason for justification because my friends were right there watching, so it couldn't be rape.

"I was always looking for justification. My rapes were done in two different ways; some forcible and others the result of manipulation, but many of the manipulation rapes were reported as assaults. Despite my pent-up anger, I never felt the need to use extreme violence or weapons and I do not ever remember writing the letter that Kathy says I did threatening to kill the girls who were going to testify against me."

He looked downtrodden as he said, "It all ended because one girl from Minnesota reported me and then others followed. I was seventeen when I was arrested. Some of my victims had more than one encounter with me, many had phoned me and written letters. I saved all those letters and that was my defense when I went to court."

Todd goes to Prison

Todd was able to avoid trial by accepting a plea deal and was sentenced to prison for sixteen years for raping eleven girls. He went to a prison that specialized in rehabilitation of sexual offenders and eventually entered a very intensive sex-offender program. He was housed in a facility that was set aside for this particular purpose. It was very tough. Up until the time he started rehabilitation he never told anyone about the humiliating and degrading sexual abuse he had endured as a child. After he confessed the abuse, he needed and was given constant reassurance that the sexual abuse was not his fault because he was a only a child.

After spending about a year in the sex-offender program, Todd had a relapse because he starting have fantasies about the female guards associated with the program. He said, "I wanted to have sex with the guards and if you are involved in a program like the one I was in you can't have these feelings without creating a dangerous situation, because you don't know if you're going to cross the line and assault a staff member. I did not tell anyone right away but, instead, kept it to myself. My fantasy was to have sex with them and they would like me and everything was glorious. I was masturbating when I had these fantasies and that made it even more dangerous.

Todd finally reported himself to the authorities, after holding onto this fantasy for an extended period of time. That made him a dangerous member of the unit. So, to his dismay, he was removed from the program."

Restorative Justice - Healing & Redemption

"Two years later I went back and remained in the sex-offender program for the full three years and finished. I learned it was up to me to make appropriate choices, to manage my anger and to understand what happened to me and why I behaved the way I did. I discovered that you actually go through a cycle before committing a sexual crime, you have a pre-buildup, a buildup, you act out, try to find justification, minimize the event and then pretend to go back to being normal. Everyone in my group was asked to think of one of our assaults and then to go back twenty-four hours prior to the assault and try to remember our thoughts, feelings, and behavior. Then we were told to come up with a general view of things that played out during all our assaults and what was going on in our minds concerning the cycle we learned about -- plus we were asked to zero in on the distortions in our minds and our core beliefs."

"I discovered that I had distorted core beliefs about women and authority. Those distorted beliefs stay deep inside you and have a major affect on your life. For example: core beliefs form in your mind early in life; like how you feel about racism, female issues, authority issues, don't trust the cops, etc. My core belief about women centered on trust. I did not trust women and believed they were not worthy of my trust. That core belief developed in my mind because of my mom. Every time she told me 'Pack up we were moving out,' we never moved out, so the end result was not trusting her to protect me. Another example of one of my core beliefs is that when I started to rape, and the victim said no, I had to be persistent because I believed that I could get her to like it and actually believed I could convince any girl to like it. Maybe not initially, but she would eventually. Many of my core beliefs were distorted."

"The sex offender program I participated in was outstanding in all respects and forced me to challenge my core beliefs. When out of prison, if I feel myself start to go to any of the stages in the cycle, I know I need to immediately talk to my therapist, my support network or my parole officer. My support network consists of guys from my sex offender group, certain family members, my girl friend, people who know me and that I feel I can talk to. Not people who say, 'Hey, I've had thoughts like that and it's no big deal.' For me, it is a big deal and it's dangerous because I have already crossed the line. So, I have to be very careful who my supporters are. I am always capable of re-offending and I have to believe that even if I don't want to. I am very conscious, all the time, of what I learned in treatment -- almost to the point of going overboard. I have not re-offended and don't intend to."

While in prison Todd took part in Restorative Justice Circles that contained surrogate victims (not his personal victims but victims of crimes by other offenders), facilitators and other sexual offenders like him. He said he and the other offenders in the circle came face to face with victims of sexual crimes and heard the pain they lived with everyday -- that experience was overwhelming and painful to him and the other offenders. This, of course, made Todd acutely aware of how his victims had suffered and he decided if he ever had the chance he needed to be accountable to his real-life victims.

Ten years following his rapes he was given that chance. One of the girls he raped asked to have a victim/offender dialogue with him. That victim was Kathy. Todd knew he needed to do this to be accountable to her for his actions." I knew the dialogue would be scary for both of us -- Kathy was terrified and so was I -- but it had a tremendous impact on me. It's one thing to hear another person's victim talk in a Restorative Justice Circle or to watch a video of a victim/offender dialogue but when you are looking at your own victim face to face and see with your own eyes the pain and agony that you have caused this person, it can be a crushing experience -- and it was for me. It was very personal, very powerful and very difficult for me to see the pain that I was responsible for causing. I am grateful to Kathy for giving me the opportunity to let her know in person how sorry I was for what I did. The experience was life-changing, transforming and had a huge impact on me. It forced me to deal with the anguish I created and the complete destruction I made of her life. I do not want to hurt anyone like that again."

Life after Prison

After serving eleven years of his sixteen-year sentence, Todd was released on parole. Two times he violated parole -- not by re-offending but because of other minor parole violations. He returned to prison, served two more years and then was released. Life outside of prison is difficult for Todd because he is a labeled sex offender. At thirty-five years of age, he finds it hard to get a job, relationships are hard to maintain and he is restricted in many ways because of his sex offender status. However, he remains very remorseful for his crimes and has never re-offended.

Right after he got out of prison the first time, he married a woman that he had a relationship with as a prisoner. She helped him get through life in prison by visiting him three times a week. Also, he called her every day and looked forward to those conversations. When he finally got out of prison, they got married and had two children right away. All this happened while he was suffering many inadequacies and insecurities and adjusting to his restricted life on the outside. She became his crutch and things between them started to deteriorate. They ended up getting a divorce that got ugly. "She attempted to have me locked up twice to keep me away from my kids even though she knew I would not abuse them," Todd said. "She knew about my past and used that information against me. I didn't really have a chance. She won custody of the kids and I'm not allowed to see them so I decided the best thing, for their sake, was to sign off on them."

Restorative Justice - Healing & Redemption

Todd recalls an incident from that marriage that left him very bitter. "My wife and I along with our two babies, went to a local Protestant church service, and purposely, went to the evening service in the middle of the week so we would not draw attention to ourselves because of my past life. Shortly thereafter, the church's pastor called my parole officer and told her that since I was a sex offender we would not be allowed to come back to his church." Todd expressed bitterness and said that he still has a lot of anger toward that church, "I am a religious person and the church rejected me from a place where anyone, even me, should be allowed. That hurt me deeply and just reinforced my belief, that I had developed in prison, that I don't belong back in society."

"There are times," he says, "when I want to go back to prison because you kinda get institutionalized and feel safer in prison. I always have to be aware of my surroundings because when I was sent to prison the story of my rapes and incarceration were in the local newspapers and many of the relatives of my victims were heard saying, 'We should have killed him when we had the chance.' So, I am often fearful. If I'm in a restaurant, I always sit facing the door."

Life has been tough for Todd and he has had a hard time functioning out of prison. Good jobs are very hard for him to find because no one wants to hire a sex offender. When he applies for a job, they "c-cap" him, which means, just by plugging his name into a computer, he is immediately identified as a sex offender. It's a huge stigma and no one seems to want to give him a chance. So getting a job is an enormous problem.

Todd said, "All of my employers, where I have managed to get hired, agree that my qualifications are good and I'm a hard worker. But when looking for jobs I am almost always shot down because I'm "c-capped." I can't work in people's homes because children are usually present. I was able to get a truck driver's license and almost got a job as a tow-truck driver, but was not allowed to take it because in that position I could possibly run into one of my victims."

He regretfully added, "I love sports but I can't play sports like basketball, for example, because that is usually played in a school gym and I'm not allowed to be around children. It's the same situation with softball. All types of schools are restricted areas for me."

"Part of the reason I returned to prison when I was first released is because life it is so hard out here. I can't blame anyone but myself but friends are hard to come by, too. People who used to know me won't speak to me and all of my so-called current friends are back at prison. I often miss them and I could play sports there. It's not all great in prison but I don't have anything like "c-cap" hanging over my head. In society, being "c-capped" controls everything including where you live, if you get a job and buy a home. The Internet gives out my name, address and exactly where I'm located. When I meet people I'm afraid to tell them my name. I thought about changing it, but found out legally I can't. But it wouldn't matter because I would still be "c-caped.'"

Todd gets a Chance for a New Life

Todd says with a bit of optimism, "About two years ago I met a women with three children and we fell in love and had a little girl together. She is now six months old."

"My baby is beautiful, a sweetie and a real bright spot in my life. My girlfriend knows all about my past and both of us and the kids have met with my parole officer and therapist. We sometimes have issues between us but we seem to be able to work through them."

When asked about his anger, Todd responded, "If I get angry I get quiet and it helps if I talk about it, when appropriate, to my girl-friend, my therapist, or my parole officer. I do have a support group made up of sexual offenders who I meet with regularly and we help each other with everyday issues."

Recently, Todd inherited the family farm after his father passed away. He had taken off three months from work to care for his father before he died and during that time he reconciled with his dad and forgave him for the abuse he endured. "My father's death helped me to grow emotionally and helped me to put in perspective how my father had affected and changed the course of my life. Also, during this time I came to grips with my bad choices and took full responsibility for them and committed myself to being a survivor."

Todd says with conviction, I would not re-offend. I am a different person than I was seventeen years ago. If I decide to back to prison, I would go to a bar, have a drink and do something stupid. That would be all it takes. Supervision sucks and living in a prison is a hard life, but sometimes living on the outside as a sexual offender is like being in a prison."

"I stay close to my family and hope to get through the next year and a half, get off parole, move to my farm, find a good job and raise my kids."

Epilogue

Todd did not rape children but raped his peer group. He did not use weapons or extreme violence but he still gets put into the same sexual offender category as child rapists and other predators because there is no differentiation in the law. He also was immersed in extensive therapy for sexual offenders for about four years, agreed to face his victim and apologized directly to her. He did his best to reassure her he would not hurt her again or hurt her family; nor would he re-offend. However, his current situation is very difficult because he often does not have enough money and can't afford a decent place to live. He feels rejected by society and believes his community does not want to give him a chance or to offer him any kind of employment.

According to Todd, that's why people -- who were prisoners at one time -- commit new crimes, so they can go back to prison, because they can't make it on the outside. Currently, he is almost a thousand dollars in arrears to the Department of Corrections because he is charged sixty dollars a month for fines while on parole. Also, he has a small mortgage on his family farm and these costs put him under constant pressure because he is very limited in ways to resolve his financial and living conditions. To him, sometimes, his situation seems hopeless even though he has been out of prison for awhile. If it wasn't for his daughter and his girlfriend, he would probably go back to prison. He said he knows many guys in prison, who returned to prison after serving their time, and they say, "You get out, can't find a job, have to pay supervision fees, have a family to care for, bills you can't pay and the pressure begins to build up -- so you re-offend and go back to prison."

Todd says people around him don't understand what kind of restrictions he has to live under. He is forced to live a lie because it would be dangerous to talk about his past to anyone except the people in his support network; so he keeps to himself, doesn't really have any friends and is afraid to contact old friends because he doesn't know what they would think. He is lonely.

Todd did inherit the family farm when his father died. The farm is located in a county which is adjacent to the one where he currently resides and until his parole is over he is required to live in that county. The law says you must live in the county where your crimes were committed. He can only visit the farm every other weekend but has requested that the court grant him permission to live on the farm before his parole is up because his girlfriend and children are living there.

He recently received some good news for a change and has a reason to be somewhat optimistic. The judge ordered the court to transition him to his farm so he could be with his six-month old daughter. Todd says he actually feels normal at the farm and his argument to the judge was that he wants to be living with his family. To him, that makes more sense for his rehabilitation back into society.

The neighbors near his farm have supported him because they knew his family. All of the neighbors actually signed an affidavit and came to court in support of him living at the family farm. The local judge was surprised and it was overwhelming and reassuring to Todd. So things are really looking better.

Todd firmly stated, "I take full responsibility for all my victims and if I could take back what I did to them I would. If I could change time, I would. They did nothing wrong. None of them. It was all my fault and I hold myself totally accountable."

Dr. Mark Umbreit, who heads the Center for Restorative Justice and Peacemaking at the University of Minnesota says, "Good victim/offender dialogue is a form of truth and reconciliation. It is not legal fact finding but it allows people's stories to come out and to be heard. To get answers to questions and to understand each other and see the humanity behind the trauma. The opportunity for reconciliation in good victim/offender dialogue is never to be pushed but it is there."

One of the major components of Restorative Justice is dialogue between the victim and the offender and the healing that comes from that ripples to family members and members of the community.

The three key jewels to getting victim involvement and offender involvement and maintaining a good process that is truly healing are preparation, preparation and preparation.

Dr. Umbreit adds, "There must be deep compassionate listening when you invite the story to surface. There must be space and time and patience for this to occur. To avoid **re-victimization** the offender must be willing to own up to his crime. Otherwise, contact with the victim should be avoided because expectations will build up that cannot be met."

When victim/dialogue is done correctly major spiritual healing can occur and the victims are often able to leave the dialogue and go back to their lives with a new directive.

As more and more Restorative Justice victim/offender dialogues are completed we know that as an outcome the offender often goes through a transforming event as well. Because our current adversarial justice system does not allow victim participation the offender never faces his victim and does not have an opportunity to try to heal the harm or right the wrong he did. When the offender participates to help his victim heal we begin to see a balance occur. This can create a paradigm shift in the way we view justice.

Survivor –Maggie
Drunk Driver –Bill

Restorative Justice
Victim/Offender Conferencing
Victim Impact Panel

*In the Restorative Justice Program in Barron County victim/offender dialogue is referred to as **victim/offender conferencing**.*

*The Heart has its reasons for
"Forgiving"
which Reason has nothing to do with.*

Maggie & Bill's Story

Maggie and her husband, Mike, were on their way to a visitation of an old friend at a local funeral home. On the way, they went through an intersection and passed what appeared to be a major automobile accident. They saw lots of cars, an ambulance and a large tractor trying to pull the car involved in the accident out of a swamp. Maggie turned around to look as they passed by and could only see the ripples on the hood of the car and noticed that it looked the same as her daughter's car. Her daughter Samantha (better known as Sam) drove a Jeep Rangler which had a grey hood with ripples.

And then it hit her -- she screamed to Mike, "That's Sam's Car." Mike tried to calm her, "Wouldn't Sam have driven through here much earlier?" Maggie thought about it and remembered that Sam was only working until one o'clock that day and agreed with Mike that she would have gone through the intersection earlier on her way home from work. So they continued on to the funeral home.

Sam worked in the special education department for the local school district and was looking forward to a short day. After work, she picked up Jackie, her eleven-month old daughter at the sitters and stopped at the grocery store in town. She then headed home and as she passed through an intersection a large pickup truck failed to stop at the stop sign. The driver, Bill -- a man in his mid-thirties -- was on his way home after working the night shift and spending the morning drinking at a local bar. His blood alcohol level was way over the limit. He was tired and drunk when he broadsided the driver's side of Sam's car at highspeed. Sam's car was so badly mangled that it took quite some time to remove her from the car. Bill was seen walking around the crash site in a daze saying repeatedly, "God, what did I do?"

Sam died instantly. Her eleven-month-old daughter, Jackie, who was strapped in a car seat on the back seat of the car miraculously survived with only a broken leg. She was removed from the car and taken to the hospital immediately by a police dispatcher who came upon the accident after almost being driven off the road herself by Bill, moments before.

Everyone was talking about the accident when Maggie and Mike arrived at the funeral home and their friends said they had called home to make sure their kids were all right. Maggie kept trying to get Sam on her cell phone. She kept calling and calling and there was no answer. Mike could see Maggie was in some distress so he suggested they leave. Maggie was feeling frightened and her intuition was working overtime. She kept thinking to herself, "It couldn't have been Sam's car. All I saw were the ripples on the hood."

As they were driving home, they went past the tire business that Sam's boyfriend Paul owned and noticed that a light was still on inside. Concerned, they decided to stop and talk to him and see if he knew where Sam was and if he knew anything about the accident.

Maggie said when she walked in, she saw a man she did not know just sitting there, so she asked him if Paul was anywhere around and he said, "No, his girlfriend was just killed in a car accident."

Maggie tearfully related, "We went to the hospital immediately, Sam was not even there yet because it was so difficult to remove her from the mangled wreck. She was dead on arrival from multiple head injuries. The doctors told us, if she had lived, she probably would never have walked again. The nurses asked if I would like to see her and I said, 'No.' Today, I occasionally regret that decision but I didn't want to remember her that way, I wanted to remember her the way she was. My wonderful, intelligent, beautiful daughter."

Maggie, Mike and Paul took little Jackie home from the hospital that evening. Her mother was dead. Now, they all had to face life without Sam whom they loved deeply. Jackie would not have a mother, Maggie and Mike lost their incredible daughter and Paul lost his loving partner and his best friend.

Sam was only thirty-one years old when she was killed. A few years before she worked as a school psychologist for a school district three or four hours from her hometown. When she became pregnant, she and Paul, her mate of fourteen years, decided they wanted to be closer to family and friends, so they moved back to Sam's hometown. She had left an excellent job and was waiting for an opening for a school psychologist in the local school district.

She and Paul had never married -- it was just not a priority, but their relationship was. Just as much of a priority to Paul was being a dad and he adored his little daughter, Jackie. After Sam's death, he was so grief-stricken he could not comprehend how he was going to live without Sam and how he was going to raise Jackie alone.

Bill receives his Punishment & Restitution

The accident occurred in Barron County, Wisconsin, in the north-central part of the state. Judge Edward R. Brunner was Circuit Court Judge at the time and was scheduled to handle Sam's case. He had just begun to implement Restorative Justice Programs in his county and he knew the affect this accident was having on the people in his local community and in the surrounding communities as well.

Everyone was very saddened by this senseless loss and outraged at the drunk driver. Maggie and her family had written a victim impact statement and they felt like everyone else did -- that Bill should be put away forever.

Judge Brunner was also personally affected by the accident. He had received an incredible number of letters telling him about the kind of person Sam was. Everyone who knew her, loved her. She dedicated her life to the care and education of children and was highly respected by her fellow professionals in the field of education. It was easy for him to derive that Sam was a lovely, outgoing, independent, hardworking and responsible person. The Judge was receiving pressure from everyone, including the press, to throw the book at Bill.

He found himself in a real quandary, "Should I send this man to prison like everyone wants me to -- or is there a more creative way to punish him and have him make restitution."

There would be no trial, just a sentencing hearing, because Bill had pled guilty. At the sentencing, the courtroom was filled to capacity with Sam and Bill's family and friends, many interested people from the community and people from the press who were ready to pounce. The tension in the room was palatable. The Judge was very aware of the scrutiny he was under, but he saw an opportunity to be fair to the family and at the same time combine punishment and restitution for Bill. Judge Brunner had a history of working with community members on cases involving divorce, domestic abuse and juvenile crime. He knew that our current judicial system was not dealing effectively with the difficult issues and needs of families, so he used Restorative Justice principles and creative sentencing to make Bill accountable.

Maggie said, "I remember that day very clearly and sitting in the courtroom listening as Judge Brunner stated, 'My job is to protect the public from any chance that Bill will ever drink and drive again. In past years, I have been known to send people to prison for this type of crime, but this time I am going to take advantage of this situation because I want to help Jackie and make this man pay for a life. Sam's family will never get over the pain, but I think they will come to realize that the vengeance or revenge derived from knowing a person is sitting in jail isn't that satisfying and it's also probably not healthy to one's psyche. Certainly, Sam did not get her attitude about life independently; she got it from her wonderful family and I have to assume that they share some of her sense of responsibility and fairness. Therefore, I sentence Bill to fifteen years in the state prison.'"

The courtroom was very quiet, you could hear a pin drop. The Judge suspended the sentence and placed Bill on probation for twenty years with a list of conditions. He warned him that failure to meet the conditions would send him to prison immediately.

The Judge ordered Bill to spend the first year of his sentence behind bars in the county jail with work privileges -- he could leave to go to work and then return to jail. The next four years he would be on electronic monitoring in his home and could only leave to go to work. As restitution to Jackie, he would be required to pay every year for the next twenty years, seventeen percent of what Sam would have made as a school psychologist.

He was also required to pay three hundred dollars a month toward Jackie's health insurance and college fund, and one hundred dollars a month toward the cost of Sam's funeral expenses. After that was paid off, the money would go into a counseling fund for Sam's family including Jackie.

Bill had made a tearful apology in the courtroom that day but the Judge insisted he also write a letter of apology to each member of Sam's family; Maggie, Mike, her two brothers and a letter to Jackie that would some day be given to her. The Judge ordered Bill to work on the letters with his probation officer. Bill was also required to visit the accident site every year on the date of Sam's death and place a memorial wreath there.

The Judge went on to tell Bill that he could not drive a car for fifteen years and if he was ever caught consuming alcoholic beverages, that would be a violation of his probation, and he would go right to prison. All of his payments would be made through the probation department and would total one thousand seven hundred and sixty five dollars a month. Bill would be paying well over half of his earnings to this little girl but he would have enough leftover to manage a meager lifestyle. He would not have to go to prison, except for the first year -- if he fulfilled all the conditions.

Bill's lawyer pointed out that the previous wages he received as a maintenance supervisor were based on overtime and in the future, because of his sentence, he might not be able to make the same amount of money. Judge Brunner responded by saying, "Well, then I guess Bill will have to get another job."

The Judge continued, "If I sent Bill to prison, Sam's daughter would have received very little in the way of a financial settlement. The amount of money that I expect Bill to pay is equal to a wrongful death action which would be three-hundred thousand dollars over twenty years. He could be sued in civil court, but since he only had twenty-five thousand dollars worth of insurance and no assets there would be little money to cover Jackie's cost of health insurance, education and support. It would not even come close to what this would provide and if Bill fails to live up to these conditions, he will have to accept the consequences."

Judge Brunner offered Sam's family an opportunity to have a victim/offender conference explaining that it was part of a program called Restorative Justice that was now being used in many states. He added, "If you do decide to participate in something like this to help with your healing, the family members involved would be offered a trained professional to aid them in the process."

Jackie's father, Paul, told the Judge, "If someone does what Bill did, that person should be ordered to take care of the survivor for the rest of their life." The Judge responded, "This is as close as I can get to that." As the sentencing hearing came to a close, Bill's attorney asked for ten minutes for him to say goodbye to his family before he reported to prison. The Judge granted his request by saying, "Alright, you can have the ten minutes to say good-bye but that's more than Sam got."

The Judge then extended his sympathy to Sam's family and told them he did his best to give them justice and tried to help Jackie at the same time.

Maggie said, "I was so thankful to Judge Brunner for everything he did for our family that day. I had never heard of Restorative Justice before the accident and we had no idea when we went to the sentencing hearing that day what was going to happen. The Judge's sentence was pretty amazing. Our family was so full of grief that we had not even had time to begin to think about how Paul was going to raise this little girl all by himself and how he was going to afford it. Sam had the bigger salary between the two of them and Paul was going to have a tough time emotionally as well as financially caring for Jackie. Of course, I would have taken her in a minute, but I knew I couldn't do that. She was all he had left of Sam. If it had not been for Judge Brunner, there are so many things that Jackie would not have today."

Jackie grows up!

Today, Jackie is ten-years of age and everyone agrees that she looks just like her mother, in fact, looking at pictures of Sam at the same age, one could say they appear identical. Maggie said with a combination of sadness tinged with a little spark in her voice, "In some ways it's like having Sam back because Jackie is so much like her mother."

"Sometimes I think it would have been easier for Jackie if she had been older when her mom died, because she would have remembered having a mother. She does understand what a mother is but she doesn't know what it's like to have one. The whole family tries to help and we talk about Sam all the time and I know her dad does too, but it is clear to me, you can never replace a mother's love no matter how hard you try."

For example, Maggie said, "when Jackie was younger and Mother's Day came around she would come home from school crying because she didn't have a mom to make a gift for, like the other kids did. But Jackie has a strong independent nature like her mom and those characteristics, I know, have helped and will continue to help her in the future.

She knows all the facts about the accident that killed her mother but I don't think she realizes yet, what a drunk driver is."

Over the past nine years since the accident, Paul and Jackie have maintained a very close relationship with Jackie's grandparents. This has kept the family together and her presence has eased some of the awful pain of loss. Maggie explained, "This Christmas turned out to be very special and so much better than previous years when Sam's loss was so agonizing. One of my sons has a special girlfriend who he brought home to join our family on Christmas Eve and Paul brought a lovely girl that he has been dating for the past year. We were all together at our home, and it was a good feeling." She said she watched Jackie respond positively to her dad's new friend and when Maggie asked her how it was going, Jackie said, "Well, OK, she's real nice but every morning I have to make my bed, and pick up my clothes." Maggie said, "I smiled silently to myself and thought, This is a good thing."

"Restorative Justice has been a wonderful gift to our family. It gave us security for Jackie's future. Of course, we lost Sam, but at least we do not have to worry about Jackie's financial needs while she's growing up. At the time of the accident, I was not even thinking about Jackie going to college, but the Judge did, and I will be forever grateful to him for that."

Maggie said she felt it was much better for Bill to be made accountable in an actual sense rather than to go to prison. Judge Brunner said at the time, "If I send this man to prison, it is not going to accomplish anything," and he was absolutely right. She added, "I realize that Bill is lacking material things that he needs today because of his financial responsibilities because I'm sure his job doesn't pay that much. Also, at the time of the accident, he did own a home but sold it because he thought he was going to prison. I'm sure thing' have been tough for him financially."

In the last several years, Maggie was in court at least two times because Bill wanted to make changes to some of his conditions. He wanted to get an occupational driver's license and she spoke against him getting that privilege. He was turned down twice. Also, he was really having to struggle to pay the two hundred dollars a month for Jackie's college fund and wanted to buy a treasury bond that would accumulate to forty-five thousand or fifty thousand dollars by the time Jackie went to college. Maggie said, "I did agree to that, but the only reason I did was because I realized that if something happened to him that money would stop. This way Jackie would always have that treasury bond. So his payments were reduced by two hundred dollars a month."

Victim/Offender Conference

About six years after the accident, Maggie approached Polly Wolner, the Executive Director of Restorative Justice in Barron County about setting up a Restorative Justice victim/offender conference. Maggie had remembered Judge Brunner offering her the opportunity during Bill's sentencing hearing when he said it could help with healing some of the pain of loss. It was appealing to think that she could release some of the pain she lived with every day, also, she had been thinking about some questions she wanted to ask Bill in a face to face situation. She said when she saw him just sitting in the courtroom, at his various court appearances, he looked like a nice young man and his mom was always there with him. "Since I had encountered him a few times in court it sorta felt like a relationship was developing between us and there were some things I needed him to know and I just simply wanted to meet him," Maggie said.

She went on to say that she believed it was important to tell him she had no bad feelings towards him and that she had forgiven him. Maggie said, I wanted to make it clear to him that I was forgiving him for myself, so I could continue the process of healing from Sam's loss." Her other family members, like Sam's brothers and Jackie's father did not want anything to do with Restorative Justice. They were still very bitter towards Bill so she avoided the subject with them hoping that some day, maybe they could learn from her experience -- if it turned out to be positive.

Polly was able to get Bill to agree to participate to a victim/offender conference. Maggie said, "It did not take that long for me to prepare because I knew exactly what I wanted to say and the questions I wanted answered." She added,"I was pretty nervous about it though."

The face to face dialogue between them went well and took about two hours to complete. Maggie asked Bill what affect the accident had on him and how things were going for him. With tear-filled eyes he said, "I am so sorry about causing your daughter's death. I carry the guilt with me every day, it never leaves me, it's always foremost in my mind." Then, when Maggie told Bill that she forgave him, he was absolutely stunned.

Bill said, "I think my heart stopped for thirty seconds when she told me she forgave me plus my whole outlook on life changed. I immediately felt my head clear a bit and I felt a little better about myself. Her statement, also, helped to propel me to go on with my life a little better than before I sat down with her. I consider Maggie to be an awesome lady."

As the conference continued, Bill tried to answer Maggie's questions as completely as he could. She asked him if he remembered the accident and he said he only remembered bits and pieces. He mentioned he had hit his head very hard during the accident and was "kinda out of it for two or three days," adding, "that was probably a good -- or maybe a bad thing." Maggie said she actually felt sorry for him because she could see how bad he felt about what he had done. She realized he would be in his fifties before he would be finished paying restitution, and he worked up to seventy hours a week to keep up his payments. "Sometimes I wonder if it was a harsher punishment to pay all that money than to go to prison, but after all he did take my daughter's life."

Maggie felt the dialogue did give her some emotional healing but it also gave her insight and understanding into who Bill was. It was clear to her that over the past seven years he had responded well to all the conditions placed on him and had tried hard to make restitution through the Restorative Justice opportunity that Judge Brunner had given him.

"I am not the type of person that carries a grudge. What Bill did was wrong and I wish Sam were here today but I knew that if he could take it back he would. The dialogue turned out to be a positive and transforming experience for both of us," she said.

Bill's reaction to his Punishment

"My sentence took everyone by surprise including me," Bill said. Obviously, I preferred it to going to jail. I certainly think I was treated fairly because paying the restitution is not the problem, the problem is living with the guilt. It's always there and never goes away and is a huge burden to carry."

He revealed he was an alcoholic and a regular attendee of AA meetings but at the time of the accident he was too arrogant to admit he had a drinking problem. When he was seventeen he started to develop a police record of DUIs (Driving Under the Influence), so alcohol was a problem for him for some time before the accident.

Bill said "People often say to me, 'There, but by the grace of God, go I.' This just clarifies to me that we live in a culture where too many people drink and drive. That needs to change so these types of accidents don't happen. I am currently involved with Barron County's Restorative Justice and Alcoholics Anonymous Program. My hope is that by sharing my experience I can make others think twice before they drink and drive. Many people just don't realize how little alcohol it takes to be over the legal limit. In Wisconsin the legal limit is .08 and a person who weighs one hundred and fifty pounds can reach that limit by just drinking three cans of beer."

Bill will be on probation until 2019 and he has great respect for Judge Brunner who gave him an opportunity to be accountable for his actions. Bill said, "What the Judge did was very meaningful to me and it gave me a chance to try to right a wrong. If a person is truly sorry, his energy can be used in a positive way. He often thinks of what would have happened to him if he went to prison and it scares him to think of what he might have become."

"If I had gone to prison I probably would have just wasted away but instead I was given a chance to do something positive for Sam's daughter. I have never met Jackie -- maybe someday -- but it will be hard for me to handle. I know the guilt will never go away and I don't expect to ever get over it, just like Maggie is never going to forget the pain of her loss. I need to face my guilt every day and to learn to live with what I did, but just knowing that Maggie doesn't hate me has helped me so much and given me a better outlook toward my life and my future."

Bill tries to get an Occupational License

Seven years after the accident Bill decided to go back into court to ask for an occupational license again -- he had already been refused twice. Maggie decided she would not contest his request if he would agree to certain conditions. She talked with the District Attorney and Polly and they decided instead of a court hearing they would hold a mediation, which is another use of Restorative Justice practices. At the mediation, they reached an agreement that Bill could have the occupational license if he would agree to pay more for college if Jackie needed it, continue making his support payments and, if he became disabled, that Jackie was to be made beneficiary of her college fund. They also required that Bill take out a life insurance policy and make Jackie the sole beneficiary. Bill agreed to all of this and then received his occupational license.

Two years later, a second victim/offender conference between Bill and Maggie was held. Maggie wanted to check on how things were going and get an update on Bill's driving privileges. During the conference, she discovered those privileges were broader than she had expected. She started to protest, but during their discussion, realized that his ability to drive was completely controlled by his probation officer. So, she decided to drop the issue. By this time she had developed a basic trust in Bill, and she felt he deserved that. He had certainly lived up to his end of the bargain by satisfying all his obligations through the Restorative Justice Programs and had agreed to all the conditions she had ever asked of him.

The conference continued on a more friendly basis and Maggie showed Bill some pictures of Jackie and shared some things with him about her. She then asked him how his mother was doing remembering how she'd always accompany Bill to court. "Your mother seems devoted to you," Maggie said. "I can just imagine how she must have felt about the accident and Sam's death." Maggie went on to suggest, "I would like to meet with your mom -- just mother to mother." Bill gave her his mother's phone number. She told him, "One of these days I am going to call her and maybe I will be able to help her with her pain."

Following that conference Maggie came to the conclusion that Bill was really a good person and did not intentionally mean for any of this to happen. He did the best he could to do everything Judge Brunner asked of him and even mentioned that he had great respect for the judge and called him, "Amazing."

Epilogue

"Losing Sam was and still is hard to bear," said Maggie. "She was a wonderful, very independent young woman and I loved her dearly. Material things were not important to her. She just wanted to see everyone happy and she always made everything special and that's why I miss her so much. I never thought that I would lose my child and I am sure most young people today, including my own sons, think that is not going to happen to them. But it can. Losing your child has to be the worse thing that can happen to anyone."

Paul has taken Sam's loss very hard. He still doesn't like to talk about it and carries around a lot of residual anger but as a father, he has done an amazing job. It has been tough for Jackie not to have a mother but she has turned into an incredible little girl and if her mom were here today she would be very proud of her. When her dad recently got a girl friend, Maggie was excited for Jackie, saying, "This could be just what she needs. Lets hope so!"

Bill continues to work long hours to keep up his payments. When asked if he feels resentful for having to pay all that money he said, "I really don't think that is the case but it was tough for awhile. I've been promoted enough in my job to eke out a meager living and lead a rather sober life. I'm able to drive now but cannot and would not drink. Also, a person convicted of a felony cannot own a firearm, that's OK, but I did love to hunt. I now own a home but don't have a family and think I'm too old to start one, but the door is not totally closed on that. Just the knowledge that Maggie does not despise me is the one thing that keeps me going plus the fact that she really understands how sorry I am for what happened."

Maggie reveals that talking about Sam and the accident actually helps her to heal and Restorative Justice has given her that outlet which has been so important to her. Through the conferences with Bill she discovered a strength she never knew she had and she no longer considers herself a victim but participates in Restorative Justice practices as a victim transformed.

She feels Polly Wolner and Judge Brunner played such an important role in her life that they feel like part of her family. She knows the Judge put a lot of thought and creativity into Bill's sentence and feels that the overall results have worked well and have certainly been to Jackie's benefit.

Restorative Justice not only positively affected Maggie and Bill but also set a clear example for the whole town. About three years after the accident, the Judge made an interesting observation. "Bill was often seen in town riding to and from work on his bike and I suddenly realized that I never had a DUI come before my bench from an employee of the company where he worked. Apparently, he became a 'case in point' of what could happen if you drink and drive. In fact, it was an example for the whole town and had an impact on many people. It was a positive thing.

Maggie added, "I was so grateful the Judge did not send Bill to prison because he secured Jackie's future and that is one thing I did not have to worry about. Because of Judge Brunner's decision Jackie has, and will be given, so many opportunities."

This story is a classic example of Restorative Justice. The victim received healing through the a victim/offender conference and the offender was made accountable to his victim and his community. Judge Brunner used his power as a judge to help the offender pay for the life he had taken. In his words, "It shows the balance than can be achieved in the proper use of Restorative Justice Practices."

Judge Brunner was asked about the truth-in-sentencing laws and how was he able to mandate this creative sentence for Bill. He responded by saying, "Any judge can do this if he wants to."

In 1998 when the Judge introduced the philosophy of Restorative Justice to Barron County and the state of Wisconsin he encouraged and supported the development of Barron County's own independent Restorative Justice Program. His most brilliant move was to stay on the side lines and let the community take control.

At the time the Board of Directors was created, Judge Brunner insisted that it be community-based and not under the auspices of the court, the prosecutor's office, law enforcement, schools or human services. This made it more of a challenge to fund.

Polly Wolner became Executive Director and she rose to that challenge and developed partnering from shareholders. She has demonstrated it's viability as a model for small communities financially and in real measurable success. Building and maintaining the trust and collaboration of the key stakeholders has been the glue which holds the program together. This requires ongoing education about Restorative Justice in the community and Polly has been able to do that for the last eight years. She does an exemplary job.

Barron County's program was one of the first in the nation and focuses primarily on juveniles. If the crime is not a violent offence, the juveniles are diverted immediately into the Barron County Restorative Justice Program. Pre-conferences occur before juvenile offenders meet with their victims and sometimes it takes time for the victims to be willing to take that step. When juvenile offenders do meet face to face with their victims the offenders are made accountable through restuition and punishment for their behavior and the harm they caused to the victims and the community. Reconciliation frequently occurs bringing healing to the victim and a balance to the process.

Juvenile crime in Barron County has been dramatically reduced since it started using Restorative Justice in the year 2000. It is a great success story and a model that many states are trying to replicate.

Barron County, also spends a great deal of time on crime prevention by using Victim Impact Panels and Restorative Justice Circles in the local schools.

After seven years in Barron County, Judge Brunner moved on to join the Appellate Court in Wausau, Wisconsin. He continues to be a passionate voice for Restorative Justice and often speaks on the subject urging other Judges to see its positive results.

Judge Brunner was awarded the William H. Rehnquist Award in

2006 for Judicial Excellence. This is one of the most prestigious judicial honors in the United States and he is only the eleventh jurist to receive this award and the first Wisconsin Judge to be so honored. He was given this award for his strong leadership with initiatives designed to instill public trust and confidence in the Wisconsin courts. His innovative initiatives, like promoting Restorative Justice, are recognized as national models.

At the end of the book is a description of the organization of Barron County's Restorative Justice Program.

Following is a commentary on a Victim Impact Panel, an explanation of how they function, why they are used and a story about one that was held in Barron County.

Victim Impact Panel

Victim Impact Panels are widely used as an effective crime prevention tool in prisons and communities throughout the nation and in various countries throughout the world. The panel usually consists of victims of crime and offenders who share their experiences with an audience of prisoners, first-time drivers, people convicted of DUIs etc. The effects on the audience can be overwhelming, life-changing and offers convincing and proven deterrents to future crime.

A Victim Impact Panel is periodically held in Barron County at the Rice Lake City Hall. Maggie and Bill whose story was illustrated on the previous pages, are active participants. All students attending driver's education programs in Barron County's high schools are required to attend and also all DUI offenders in the county. Teenage attendees must be accompanied by a parent or another adult.

The audience often has about one hundred people in attendance and Barron County's Victim Impact Panel usually consists of Maggie who lost her daughter Sam; Anne and Larry whose seven-year-old son was killed in a car accident because his father drove while intoxicated; Mary, whose eight-year-old son was killed by a drunk driver when getting off the school bus; plus, via video tape, Keith, who is imprisoned for fifteen years, because, while driving under the influence, he caused a three-car accident that resulted in the death of two people and injury to a third person.

Panel members who have lost loved ones tell their stories of loss, and the drunk drivers tell their stories of causing the loss.

There usually is not a dry eye in the room as this is happening. The stories are incredibly moving and words cannot be found to describe the pain everyone in the audience feels as they listen intently to how lives can quickly be destroyed by a person who drinks and drives.

Keith looks like the guy next door and always stuns everyone with his incredibly sad story about destroying his life by just drinking three beers.

Anne talks about the death of her eight-year old son because her husband was drunk when he drove her two boys home from a family party. He was by himself and only had to drive two miles; so he put both boys in the back of his pickup truck. The truck went off the road into a ditch and his eight-year old son was killed. She explains how hard it was to forgive her husband and go on with her life. Her husband, Larry, always -- "blows everyone's mind"-- as he plays the 911 tape of the emergency phone call he made to get help for his son. He was so drunk he could not give directions to his location as his son lay dying.

Mary speaks about trying to revive her eight-year old son after he got off the school bus and was hit by a drunk driver. She describes the sadness she lives with every day without her son.

Restorative Justice – Healing & Redemption

Maggie, from our previous story, talks about losing her daughter, Sam. She tells everyone that after Sam's death, she found a letter on Sam's computer written to her baby daughter, Jackie. Maggie read the letter to everyone and it follows:

Jackie, there is so much I want to tell you, I have thought about this letter a lot but have just finally begun to put it down into words today. You have to know first and foremost that I love you. I could never have imagined how how much a person can love until you were born. From the day that I found out that I was pregnant I have loved you. I was so excited when I found out that I would finally be a mother. I had dreamt of it for some time. I think I knew all along it would be a girl. I wanted a girl but did not want to get my hopes up. The important thing to me was that my child would be healthy and you were. You weighed seven pounds eleven and a half ounces. You have been in my life for a bit less than five months, but I could not imagine my life without you. I read once that having a child is like your heart walking around outside your body. So true. Losing you now is my biggest fear. However, I don't think of that. Already, you have had a tremendous impact on my life. It is you that takes up the majority of my thoughts and time. I hate leaving you in the morning and can't wait to be home to see you each evening. I picture your smile, your laugh, your touch. I can smell your baby smell and feel you in my arms all snuggly and safe.

When the panel finishes and as the audience files out -- many stop to express their sorrow to the panel members.

The members, who have been doing this together for quite some time, always gather together afterward in a smaller room at City Hall. They call each other family and express the fact that they could not have gotten through all the pain they've experienced without each other. They usually need to take some time to compose themselves from all the emotion they have expressed telling their stories. It seems rather unusual to find survivors and offenders hugging each other and offering support and forgiveness after having expressed their incredibly painful stories. The room is filled with a palatable feeling of love and caring for each other and anyone witnessing their interaction would find it to be an overwhelming experience. The whole process expresses the epitome of Restorative Justice because of the devotion the panel has for one another. It truly is a coming together of victims and offenders sharing their pain and offering healing to each other. Watching all this play out can make a person wonder, if, as it is often stated, that the worse experience that can happen to a person is to lose a child; but, could being responsible for the death of another's child be as painful or very close to that same kind of pain?"

The members say that it helps them to participate in the Victim Impact Panel because if they can get just one person not to drink and drive then their loved one did not die in vain. The drunk drivers hope to stop people from doing what they did. Speaking at the panel gives them a purpose, relieves some of their horrific guilt and is part of their restitution. The survivors and offenders are really united in their motivation to stop drinking and driving. This purpose unites them with a bond that's hard to explain. It takes tremendous courage to share the pain of their experiences no matter what side of the issue you are on -- survivor or the offender. The experience of attending a Victim Impact Panel and getting involved in Restorative Justice can widen the vision of what people can do to help each other.

JJ – Murderer

Restorative Justice Circles

*We cannot hide the truth
about ourselves, from ourselves*

JJ's Story of Murder

It was a beautiful sunny day, blue sky with warm summer breezes and JJ had just finished his sophomore year in high school with straight A's. He and two of his friends slowly walked toward his dad's home where he would spend the summer. His dad ran a crackhouse. When he arrived he could see what he already knew: There was no change in his father, he was always inert, uncommunicative and gone on crack. You know, really not there at all. The electricity at the house had been turned off because no one ever paid the bill.

JJ's thoughts centered on what he had to look forward to during his summer vacation. Actually, nothing. After working hard at the Catholic school he attended he now faced the reality of spending the summer where no one really cared about him. He later described his feelings that day as despondent; everything seemed hopeless, out of control, and he didn't really care about anything and felt like giving up."

Bob, a hard-core drug user and the man who had started his Dad on crack, sauntered into the house that afternoon swinging a bag of money. Big money, that he had scammed from people. JJ's immediate thought was that money could turn the electricity back on and, maybe, he could have a life this summer after all.

JJ grabbed the arms of his two buddies and told them to follow him to his room where they got high on drugs and booze while devising a plan to rob Bob of the money. They left the house, located a gun from a friend who was a gang member, loaded it and returned to the house. Then the three of them confronted Bob and JJ pointed the gun at him, rather shakily, and demanded the money. Bob mocked them while smoking more crack and off-handedly said, "Get out of here you little motherfuckers. You can't have this money."

JJ was afraid of Bob, as well as humiliated by him, ever since he had attempted to rape him. Now, the humiliation combined with fear intensified. Bob's level of mocking increased and began to turn to anger and JJ was beginning to get frightened and felt himself losing control. When Bob lunged for the gun, JJ closed his eyes and pulled the trigger. Bob was killed instantly.

The three boys ran from the house and went in three different directions. In a panic, JJ dropped the gun in front of a neighboring garage and ran on. After running several blocks he remembered he had forgotten to pick up the money, so he ran back to retrieve it and left again, running faster. For some reason he thought to pick up the gun he had dropped and threw it in a nearby river.

At some point, he sneaked into his grandma's house that was a few blocks from his dad's. During the school year he lived there with his mentally-ill mother and alcoholic grandmother. He quickly took a shower and climbed into bed and went to sleep. The next day he was in a daze -- almost forgetting what had happened the day before. He walked out the front door and started down the sidewalk.

Unfortunately for him, one of his cohorts had ratted on him so he did not get far. Soon he heard someone yell "freeze." He started to run again and got caught on a fence. The police grabbed him and pommelled him forcefully. "I could hardly walk after they got through with me," JJ said. He was taken to the police station for interrogation which lasted about two days. Because of the large amounts of drugs and alcohol he had consumed sometimes he actually got sleepy. This really "ticked off" the police. One of them started choking him which eventually resulted in JJ's confession to the murder. He was then booked into the juvenile detention center. So, at fifteen year's of age, JJ, the honor student found himself charged with murder and assigned a defense attorney.

JJ is Tried and Convicted of Murder

Bob's murder occurred in 1997, making JJ one of the first juvenile cases in the state where he lived to be charged as an adult. In the 1990s nearly every state in the union decided young offenders should be tried as adults thus making it easier for judges to sentence them as adults. The age of criminal majority was dropped for juveniles from eighteen to seventeen and for the charge of murder the majority was dropped to ten years of age. This was part of the new nationwide attitude, "Get Tough on Crime."

JJ found himself charged with first degree intentional homicide which is the worst possible charge in a murder case. A plea bargain was offered -- sixty years with no chance of parole -- he and his attorney decided to take their chances with a jury trial where he might have an opportunity to reduce the length of his sentence.

Six months following his arrest the trial began. The jury was looking at a blond-haired, fair-skinned child, not very tall in stature and straight from a poverty-ridden area of one of our nations teeming cities. For conviction, the jury would be required to agree that JJ acted with the intent to kill.

The defense's strategy was to attempt to get JJ convicted of a lesser charge of murder. The law at the time stated that if a juvenile is not convicted of his original charge he can then be treated as a juvenile. This would give JJ the possibility of being sentenced as a juvenile, enable him to spend his sentence in a juvenile facility and then be released at the age of twenty-five. The big difference between the juvenile and adult criminal systems in cases of murder, is that the juvenile system is designed for the eventual release of the criminal but the adult system is designed so they are never released.

There is a clause referring to self-defense included in the charge of first-degree intentional homicide. This clause indicates that if you feel like you are in great danger of bodily harm or injury you have the right to self-defense. The judge and prosecutor agreed that in this case, this clause should be removed from the intentional homicide charge. The defense attorney fought against that throughout the trial. JJ did admit his guilt during the trial but always maintained that self-defense was involved. His attorney agreed and supported him by saying to the jury, "JJ performed an impulsive act inspired by fear."

At the end of the trial the jury was given a choice of four verdicts: guilty of intentional homicide, guilty of felony murder, guilty of reckless homicide or not guilty. The jury found him guilty of reckless homicide. There were two important parts of that verdict: First, he was not found guilty of the original charge which gave him the possibility of going into the juvenile system and Second: reckless homicide offered leniency in the time he would be required to serve. The maximum sentence is forty-five years but it could be as little as five years. JJ, of course, did not know what his sentence would be but perceived his situation was looking a bit better.

A month later, JJ found himself at his sentencing. He would have a chance to make his case for a lighter sentence and he was hoping to be treated as a juvenile. Both he and his attorney agreed he was not innocent but that there was a self-defense aspect to the crime including negligence and recklessness. During the sentencing he was supported by Brother Bob from the Catholic high school he attended and by an auxiliary bishop from his hometown. He also received support from average citizens who believed he should not be treated as an adult.

When his victim's family had their chance to speak at the sentencing, Bob's mother had a haunting effect on JJ. "I don't want JJ to be put away forever, I just want him to pay for what he did, she softly said. "Bob was not a perfect person but he did not deserve to die this way." This statement had a powerful effect on JJ. He became very emotional when he said, "It felt like some small drop of forgiveness was coming my way because she wasn't asking for me to be sent away forever. Looking back on that moment, today, I realize that to offer me any kind of forgiveness was unbelievable. I was pretty shocked. It turned out to be the beginning of my belief in what I would later come to know as Restorative Justice."

The judge went into deliberations and JJ whispered the Lord's Prayer. When the judge returned he sentenced him to twenty years in an adult prison and justified the tough sentence by saying it was the severity of the crime and the fact that he went back to get the money. The judge also commented that JJ could have just left the situation but he didn't, so he would not be treated as a juvenile but would be serving hard time. JJ described his reaction, "When you are only fifteen you cannot comprehend or imagine what twenty years of hard time in a prison would be like. I had no idea what was in store for me but I knew enough to be terrified, and I sensed that I had reason to be."

JJ's Life in Prison

JJ was immediately removed from the juvenile detention center and transferred to the county jail. In summing up his reflection on that experience, he said, "I learned quickly that county jail was like 'Jihad' and the worst jail time you could ever serve because everyone was fighting their own particular cases and were all stressed out. The tension was high and I felt like I was in the middle of a nightmare."

A large group of prisoners, including JJ, were sent to the northern part of the state to an assessment center. Since it was 1997, there was a huge influx of inmates because of the new "tough on crime" laws. One of the ways to solve the issue of overcrowded prisons was to ship many prisoners out to Texas, and JJ firmly decided he would try and use all his capabilities not to go there. When it was his turn for his assessment he pushed the fact that he was a minor and -- lucky for him -- it was decided that he could stay in his home state until he was eighteen. He ended up in a maximum-security prison -- not so lucky, and when he arrived, he was told to try to accomplish four tasks: finish his high school education, take vocational training, participate in an anger management course and complete a drug and alcohol program. JJ said he felt unsafe every day at the prison, nicknamed Gladiator School, and the average age for an inmate was twenty-one years of age.

"Everyone was buck wild," he said. Most of the inmates had very long sentences and didn't really care about anything or anybody. It wasn't long before JJ got into a fight and was sent to the hole (isolation) for seventy-eight days. Usually, you spend your time in the hole alone but since the prison was so overcrowded he had a roommate for part of the time. The hole was a tough experience for him, nothing to do, little to read and constant noise from the three hundred prisoners outside his door.

With that awful experience behind him, JJ decided to stay away from the drugs and gangs in prison. Instead, he got actively involved in prison life by taking his assigned anger-management course and getting his GED, which he quickly earned, but was required stay in the school facility until he was eighteen. While there, he got to know an amazing teacher named Miss Vandermark, who was in charge of a course called "Challenges and Possibilities." It was a six-week course and ended with a Restorative Justice Circle of victims, offenders and community members.

JJ had heard the long-timers and lifers, who were never going to get out of prison discussing this course and they told him it gave them a different perspective and a new way of looking at their life. JJ explained, "When you have lifers endorsing something in prison it usually gives it credibility." So he checked it out and decided that it sounded like something he wanted to be part of.

The lifers also recommended another group to him called "Brick." This program tries to build relationships between prisoners and inner city, at-risk kids in an age range of ten through seventeen. The kids came to prison to listen to inmates speak about their lives and how they turned to a life of crime with the hope that the kids would be deterred from making the same mistakes. Miss Vandermark was also the coordinator of "Brick." JJ made the decision to become part of this group, too. These two decisions turned out to be advantageous to him because it placed him in the company of many people who were trying to make a difference in the lives of prisoners.

JJ Discovers Restorative Justice

The Restorative Justice movement was just beginning to take hold in the United States when JJ signed up for "Challenges and Possibilities." The course had just added a Restorative Justice component and he was one of the first prisoners to experience this expansion. The first part of the course was held in a classroom and focused the prisoners' attention on the rippling effect of their crimes. It was explained to them how their crime caused pain and suffering to many people, particularly, their families and the families of their victims. Many of them had never considered the number of people they had hurt. They were all shocked and sobered by the ripple effect. Miss Vandermark also encouraged them to examine other specific aspects of the crimes they had committed.

The last three days of the class were set aside for a Restorative Justice Circle that would contain victims, offenders and members of the community. It was facilitated by Professor Geske of Marquette Law School, who was a former Wisconsin Supreme Court Judge and a passionate advocate for Restorative Justice. She arrived at the prison along with surrogate victims of crimes and members of the community. She had a piece of broken glass to be passed around the circle and whoever held the glass would be allowed to speak and everyone else must be silent and listen. By following this procedure respect would be shown to whoever was speaking. This was necessary because the circle was to be considered sacred. Then, JJ stated, "Professor Geske literally 'blew us all away' by sitting down in the circle between two hard-core prisoners. Nobody ever does that. She had guts." Also, it did not take long for the word to spread among the prisoners in the circle that one of the long-timers present had been sentenced by Professor Geske when she was a judge. "We all were blown away one more time," JJ exclaimed. "The guy was a Native American dude and was the quiet type, but had become very animated when she arrived."

Professor Geske began by introducing everyone in the circle and explained how it would function for the next three days. Then two women victims were introduced as rape victims and Professor Geske gave one of them the piece of glass to start. Her name was Sally and she was a fairly well-known rape victim in the state. She began by talking about her rape and what affect it had on her. Adding "I was also raped as a child by a neighbor that was babysitting me, but I never told anyone about the first rape until my second experience."

"My family, and I were on vacation and one bright sunny afternoon I went running on the beach and was brutally raped, beaten and left for dead," Sally said. "By some miracle, I managed to survive." She told everyone in the circle about the incredible pain this event had on her both physically and mentally. JJ said he would always remember how she described the effect on her small son. "The rape could not be hidden from my children because of the severe beating I received," she said. "Soon my little son began drawing very graphic pictures of himself trying to kill my attacker, plus, my husband had trouble controlling his rage toward the offender and kept screaming he was going to kill the guy."

JJ said, "You could feel the emotions in the room. The inmates all had wives and girlfriends and they started to relate to her on a level they never thought about when they were committing crimes similar to her rape and beating. Her story opened up a lot of inmate's minds who were in the circle. Most offenders were lifers, with no possibility of parole and these guys were really touched and backed down by Sally who was only five feet two inches tall. The emotion was just knocking these guys out. She also talked about the anguish she bore because the rapist did not take any responsibility for what he did."

Sally emphasized that every day something happened to trigger the memory of her rape and feelings of terror would return. She never goes out alone at night or never jogs on the beach. There are certain things she simply cannot do because of her rape experience. "She never gets parole," JJ sadly reiterated.

The power of her story and what the rape did to her and her family along with the ripple effect it had on her extended family and friends was overwhelming to all the circle members but particularly the offenders. JJ said, "She helped us understand, from personal experience, how the ripple effect works. She made it clear that it would not just be felt by her family but it would also affect our families too. All the offenders started to realize how many people their crimes had affected in a negative way. They were overcome with emotion. There was dead silence in the room and the offenders' eyes were full of tears. You could tell the prisoners were looking at her story from a totally different perspective and it was turning their lives upside down. Two of the prisoners had served twenty-five years and they had never thought about what their victims felt like and what they had to live with after they were raped by them."

"JJ started to think of his mother and grandmother and Bob's family and realized the extension of the ripple affect he had created. He never thought of this before this course and it had a profound affect on him.

The victims spoke on the first two days of the circle and on the third day the offenders spoke. As they went around the circle, each offender who held the piece of broken glass was allowed to speak. Some of them talked about their crime, some talked about their families, but they all said that they had never really understood how their crime had affected their families and community by way of the ripple effect.

When the piece of glass was passed to the Native American, all the offenders were very nervous wondering what he was going to say because he never talked to anyone. He held the piece of glass and looked intently at Professor Geske and asked her if she remembered him. She said, "No." He turned in her direction and loudly blurted out, "You sentenced me to forty-five years in prison and for the last few days I have been fighting with myself whether to take a swing at you." He was just being honest but the guards who were present were getting very uptight and grabbing their walkie talkies. He went on to say, "You know, I think you did the right thing. I was out of control and getting high all the time. My life was on a destructive path and I was destroying myself and others. Of course, I don't think I should have been given such a long sentence but I sure needed to spend some time looking at my life."

This came from a guy with a forty-five year sentence. JJ commented, "I didn't know how much more time he had to serve but I do know he was sincere. He didn't say it because of the program or because he wanted to get out of prison, he said it because he really meant it." That is what the prisoners call "a break" and means the prisoner accepts his life for what it is and tries to determine how he is going to change it for the better.

There was another guy in the circle, who had been, if not the leader of a gang he was at least a high-ranking member. His sentence was sixty-five years. He was black, bald-headed, looked like a fifty-year old grandfather, and JJ knew him to be one of the most respected guys in the prison. When it came time for him to speak he looked around the circle at everyone and said, "You know, I sold dope all my life, shot people and I've been shot. I did all this bad stuff. My kids hardly know me as their father. What it boils down to is I just stopped caring and that's why all of you lived lives of crimes too, because you stopped caring."

Later, at the end of the day, he confided in the rest of us who had been in the circle with him; "When I was twelve or thirteen I was raped." For a man who was a respected prisoner and a previous high-ranking gang member to admit his rape as a child was very unusual. Plus this was not his normal style -- he was really a huge guy about six feet two inches tall and probably weighed about two hundred and fifty pounds. He finally broke down and cried and told us, "For some reason, I was just driven to do a lot of what I did."

JJ said, "For a lot of the guys, the Restorative Justice Circle was the first time they had ever come face to face with victims and what they had done and they often broke down. After the circle program, it was routine to do prison counts more closely, because of possible suicide attempts."

When it was JJ's turn to speak about his crime, he had a tough time verbalizing his feelings because he lacked the maturity level to handle the situation and was unable to indicate how accountable he now feels. He did give a general picture of his crime, but no specifics. However, the experience of taking the course," Challenges and Possibilities," and participating in the Restorative Justice Circle forced him to think more about his victim and to look outside of himself and reflect on his actions. He realized what he had done had affected his family as well as his victim's family. "What I did had a huge ripple effect and knowing this made a big difference in my life as I began to accept all the consequences of my actions. I had never had contact with anyone from my victim's family but meeting other victims of crime had been a very powerful experience. Powerful enough to create real change in me." The Restorative Justice Program had a penetrating and powerful affect on JJ. It changed his life, and his attitude took a dramatic turn for the better.

JJ takes Advantages of Opportunities

In prison if you do what you are supposed to do you get rewarded. At JJ's original assessment he had been given four major programs to complete and he had managed to complete three: his GED, vocational training, and an anger management course but he did not have the opportunity to complete the drug and alcohol program. He put that "on the back burner" and decided to try networking in an effort to get some kind of job.

He went to church every Sunday and tried to make friends with some of the prison attendees. It was a sparse group, only seven guys. JJ did become friends with one of them who was a lifer. "I never met anyone who had as strong a faith as he did and he tried to help me out when he could. Because of him I was given a job in maintenance as a plumber's assistant and getting that job made a big difference in my daily life at prison and my future." JJ settled into his job figuring he would be there for a very long time; he kept busy, tried to do his best, discovered he was good at fixing things and always helped during clean up. He was also tutoring prisoners for Miss Vandermark. Because of his good behavior and good attitude he started to get noticed by the many people he came in contact with while doing his various chores.

The education director at prison knew JJ had high test scores and he was hearing very positive comments about him, but he also knew he was facing a long sentence. He started to look into JJ's case file and discovered the one thing he had not accomplished was his drug and alcohol program. The director decided he would rectify that. So, after spending five years in a maximum-security prison, JJ was sent to a medium-security prison with triple razor wire fences instead of walls. There, he became part of a braille transcription program, making books for blind children. The braille program was profitable for the prison because of inexpensive labor costs and, at the same time, it provided a service to the community by helping the blind.

The braille transcription job was very tough and JJ would need a year of training before he could actually begin making books, but he knew this was a great opportunity because he was acquiring a usable skill plus making restitution by giving back to the community. He had really enjoyed his job as a plumber's assistant but knew he needed to accept this change in his life because he was being offered more freedom and more opportunities. In many ways things were looking better and he was not as locked-in and had more physical freedom. He was allowed to be more active by playing his favorite sport, basketball, and that helped his transition and his perspective.

JJ made text books for two years and was also very involved with Catholic Services at the prison. He always went to church and the chaplain recruited him to help with the masses. Through that connection he discovered a program called "Victim Impact" which was similar to his previous prison's program "Challenges and Possibilities." This program was another interpretation of Restorative Justice built on the same philosophy -- victim/offender dialogue and the ripple effect.

The culminating point in "Victim Impact" was a lot like" Challenges and Possibilities" because the prisoners met the victims and/or survivors at the end of the course. JJ was delighted to meet Sally again. She told him she makes the rounds of the prisons trying to heal herself and heal others at the same time. In this particular program there were about twenty guys who signed up and when the victims showed up three dropped out. "I felt the reason they left was because they could not face the victims," JJ recalled soberly. "I also believe these three are most likely to re-offend because they could not take full responsibility for their actions. Most of guys who stayed 'broke,' just like the other prison. They broke down and hit rock bottom when they had to come face to face with victims." Along with Sally there were other rape victims who were very strong women. They talked about the kind of life they live and how they struggle to return to some type of normalcy. Everyday something will trigger awful memories of their rapes.

At this medium-security prison, JJ was also participating in a group like the one called "Brick." He, like some of the lifers, often spoke to groups of kids. Here, the prison didn't just bring in the kids who were at risk but would bring in a whole class of middle school and high school students. The focus was not to scare the kids into not wanting to go anywhere near a prison but to train the kids to think before they acted and to understand the consequences.

JJ added, "We discussed different aspects of our stories with the kids probably more about where we started from than where we ended up. Most of the lifers had been in prison for twenty-five or thirty years and it was interesting for me to hear their individual stories and what it was like when they were teenagers. I was amazed to discover that the stories from the younger guys and the older guys were almost identical because they included the same elements -- no parental support, bad friends, bad decisions, drugs and alcohol. We really were able to connect with these kids and hopefully made a difference in their lives."

Since I was involved in similar programs that I had been in before and was also busy making books for the blind, I met many different types of people. I knew that was a positive omen and I often felt God was watching over me and I tried to keep my faith strong and be optimistic about my future."

JJ is Shocked, he gets Paroled

JJ was now close to having spent seven years in prison having served five at the maximum-security facility and now almost two in the minimum-security prison. He was not expecting anything exciting to happen. He had met with the parole board during his fifth year, as a formality, and his parole was automatically denied. At that time, he was given a forty-eight month deferment, which meant that he would not see the parole board again for four years. That was OK with him and he did not feel he could anticipate anything else. He was just pleased with how things were going.

One day "out of the blue," JJ got a letter saying he was going to be up for parole review in twenty-four months. This was highly unusual! He wondered how this had happened and went to the parole office to find out. When he got there, they gave him an endorsement to take the drug and alcohol program because that was the only thing left on his to-do list. He had finished everything else from his initial assessment. To get into that program is often very difficult he said because it is usually selective and reserved only for the guys getting out. "I took the endorsement and forced myself not to read anything meaningful into it."

As it turned out it meant everything! He was removed from braille transcription and immediately sent to the drug and alcohol program. Every day for four months he attended a very intensive group program about addiction. After that was finished, he was given a form indicating that he had a chance at parole. JJ couldn't believe his good fortune and said, remembering his excitement, "This whole procedure was out of the ordinary. Normally I would have gone from a medium-security prison to a mimimum-security prison but the braille program had put a hold on me to keep me there because I was making money for them, doing a good job and not being a behavior problem. I didn't know about the hold. I was shocked. Because of the hold I was allowed to go from maximum to medium then right into the community. I was quite surprised and thrilled by all this."

On the thirty-first of May, the parole commissioner sent JJ an official letter stating that he was being paroled because of his excellent progress, the different programs that he had attended, the fact that he did not have any behavior problems and because of his age.

Since he was allowed to skip time in a minimum-security prison he would go directly to a halfway house. "The halfway house would be my transition back into the community." he said.

JJ left prison on the Tuesday after Labor Day. When you have been a prisoner as long as he had been, it was customary for his fellow prisoners to walk you out. They walked him as far as they could and then he went the rest of the way on his own. All his stuff was in boxes and his mom was in her car waiting for him. He said, "I walked out the door and it slammed behind me. I was intentionally still wearing my greens (prison garb) because I wanted to remember what it was like to be in prison and who I had harmed. I was twenty-three years old, and after serving almost eight years in prison, I was free. I turned and looked at the prison, for the first time, from the outside."

JJ and his mom had only driven for a short time when he asked her to pull over because he was going to be sick. He immediately started throwing up. The most prominent thought in his mind was that he had to report to his parole officer in his hometown by two p.m. and he had no idea where the officer was located and if he was going to make it in time. His mom had him confused because she kept saying, "We're going to have this great meal because it's your first night of freedom." His head was spinning. "It was the most miserable ride of my life but I was free. I think I threw up in every town on the way home. We actually made it to the parole office one hour ahead of time and my parole officer told me I had to report to a residential-treatment center immediately. She put me in the back seat of her car and I felt like I was going back to prison -- no handcuffs -- but I did not even get a chance to say goodbye to my mom."

JJ was in the residential-treatment center for ninety days. There were no bars on the windows or doors, he said, but it felt like prison. After three days he was allowed to go on a job search and soon discovered that his friend, Brother Bob, had a job waiting for him in the bookstore at the Catholic high school he had previously attended. Brother Bob had spoken up for him at his sentencing hearing and had stayed in constant contact with him during the last eight years.

JJ was allowed to leave the center and work during the day and Brother Bob would visit him on Sundays and bring Communion. Every day when he returned from work he would have to blow into a breathalyzer and have a urine test done to make sure he was not using drugs or alcohol. He said, "The residential treatment center was the worst excuse for treatment I had every seen. More of the guys got high in the treatment center than in prison. I could not figure out how they didn't get caught. Made no sense to me. I had a roommate who was drinking and I was terrified he was going to get caught and would somehow blame me. I was so glad to get out of there, it was almost worse than prison because it was out of control."

JJ is so Grateful to Brother Bob

JJ became very emotionally when he spoke about what Brother Bob had done for him. He said, "I feel so indebted to him and I will never forget what he did for me. When I was in the maximum-security prison, he visited me whenever he could and during the entire eight years I was in prison, he wrote to me every single week and sometimes twice a week. When I was in the medium-security prison he visited every month. He had always been there for me, from the very beginning, telling the police that I could not have done this murder because I was an outstanding student and that he was sure they had the wrong person. Brother Bob was my biggest supporter, writing to me, visiting me and sending me books. He was my rock when everyone else was gone and I was not that surprised when my parole officer mentioned that Brother Bob had offered to provide a place for me to live."

The Catholic high school that JJ had attended was an independent school not connected to a parish and the property also had a house on it. JJ was allowed to live there rent free for three months and was given a job in the school's bookstore. After the three months were up, he was charged a low rent because he worked on weekends and kept an eye on all of the school property.

He said that Brother Bob told everyone, "I am going to give this young man a legitimate chance to make it -- three pillars: a place to live, a place to work and spiritual support."

And that is exactly what he did, JJ said. "Brother Bob was connected to many community programs so I had a lot going for me. I am convinced that part of the reason I was released was because of his incredible support."

Brother Bob insisted that JJ continue his education. When he asked how he was going to pay for it, Brother Bob told him not to worry about it. Shortly, thereafter, JJ discovered that he could get financial aid and grants to pay for his education. So to get started he took a class at an area tech school while working full-time. The class was easy for him. Brother Bob suggested he apply to a nearby college which he did and was accepted. His first and second year were paid for by grants because he was living below the poverty level. He did well in college, made the Dean's list, was a 4.0 student and double majored in English and Education. One of the issues that concerns him is that when you are on parole, and he will be until the year 2017, you are not allowed to purchase anything on credit, which includes student loans. This will soon become a real problem for him, but, JJ has made it this far so it is doubtful that this will deter him. He will find a way.

His goal is to become a teacher and he has been made aware of the huge mountain he will have to climb because he is a convicted murderer. "Only drug and sex offenses prohibit you from becoming a teacher, but getting certified may be a huge problem," JJ said. I am keenly aware that I may never be allowed to teach but am looking at other ways to get around that by getting a Masters and/or a Doctorate degree and teach in a college."

He is willing to take the chance and helps his situation by tutoring and mentoring kids as well as holding a full-time job while being a full-time student. He is driven to make his life a success.

JJ has a Survivor/Offender Dialogue

When JJ is asked about his victim he tells the story of accidentally getting the opportunity to talk to his victim's daughter through email. He said. "When I first got out of prison I was very busy with work and school but rather quickly I got up to speed on all the new technology and started my own 'My Space' page -- I thought it was so cool. I told my personal story on my 'My Space' page and somehow my victim's daughter found it. She emailed me and asked if I was the person who killed her father. I replied by telling her who I was and asking if she would like to go on instant messenger and discuss it with me. So, that's what we did. She said her name was Susan and she was Bob's daughter who no one knew about and she lived out west. She had some brutally honest questions to ask. First, she wanted to know if there were any good things about her dad. She asked that question more than once and added that her mom never had anything nice to say about him. She also wanted to know what his last moments were like." JJ knew, because of his training in Restorative Justice, to be very sensitive and careful what he said to her. He tried to answer her questions as honestly as he could but with a great deal of tact.

He told her that her dad was a very handy person, worked well with his hands and made great pancakes. "We chatted back and forth for about two hours. She seemed to have a genuine curiosity about her father and was not expressing any bitterness," JJ said. He could tell she was looking for some kind of closure because she was about to be married and it seemed she wanted to put her father issue to rest and close that chapter of her life and move on.

He knew that he was taking a risk talking to her because a parolee is not allowed to have contact with his victim's family without permission. It turned out his parole officer was very understanding about the conversation because JJ had printed it all out and gave her a copy. She just told him not to do it again and to take his "My Space" page down and not to advertise his background. He did not have any more contact with her but gave her email address to his parole officer.

"Honestly, I don't expect to hear from her again, I think I've answered all the questions she was searching for. The Restorative Justice programs that I participated in prepared me for this encounter with my victim's survivor and I certainly knew enough not to tell her that her father was just a dope addict," JJ said. "Before this email exchange I didn't know she existed and I don't know if Bob had more children. I do know he had a sister but don't know if she is still living. I won't search for members of my victim's family but if they want some type of dialogue I would be open to it."

Epilogue

JJ's story is very compelling and has a wonderful ending which is really a new beginning for him. He now has a car and is working full-time and going to school full-time. His future is bright. He will be on parole until 2017 and during that time he cannot drink alcohol or get involved with drugs, and, he will have to be very cautious about his behavior for the next nine years. He is very confident he can handle that after what he has been through.

He sincerely believes that Restorative Justice made all the difference for him. "When my victim's mother, who testified at my sentencing hearing, offered me something pretty close to forgiveness -- something I never thought I would have or deserved, that was the spark that turned me in the right direction. Then the Restorative Justice Circle with Professor Geske was such a profound and unforgettable experience for me personally, because I actually witnessed other prisoners 'break.' All this made me a believer in the power of Restorative Justice."

JJ has actually spoken to students in some of Professor Geske's classes at Marquette Law School. He tells them about his prison time and his direct experience with Restorative Justice and how it changed his life, his perspective, and his attitude.

Professor Geske has been going to the same maximum-security

prison twice a year for the last nine years doing Restorative Justice Circles. Each circle lasts for three days and includes offenders along with surrogate victims, members of the community and facilitators. In the circle, the offender is in a different role then everyone else because he/she made the choice to commit a crime and is the one who must be held accountable.

The first day of the circle they spend getting comfortable with each other by doing different exercises and Professor Geske explains to the offenders about the ripple affect of their crimes. She often gives the following example: "When a child is kidnapped from their bedroom in California tonight -- tomorrow the kids in Maine are afraid to go to sleep in their bedroom, that is the ripple effect. Crime not only affects the people directly impacted by the offender but it can affect us all."

On the second day hours are spent listening to the victims tell their stories; what their life was like before the crime, the gruesome details of what happened to them and how it changed their lives and their family's lives. The evening of the second day the offenders are introduced to the ripple affect and what happened to the families of their victims and then, usually for the first time, they think about their families and how their crime affected them. They get very emotional. On the third day they share their feelings with the circle. The experience of having to face what they did by looking into the eyes of a victim like theirs is overwhelming.

This whole process has a unique quality embedded in its midst because most of the offenders are victims themselves. The offenders can identify with the victims -- but as offenders they never got beyond their rage of being a victim which is why they inflict that rage on innocent people. Slowly this important connection solidifies and they become aware of its impact. They are both victims -- this has a powerful affect.

Professor Geske says, "The whole experience is always almost too much for the offenders and they get weepy and regretful for what they did. They are not allowed to contact their victim. That can only happen if the victim initiates it. They can't expect forgiveness but they can learn to forgive others and together we talk about personal things they can do. We tell them we all make mistakes and no one can change what they've done but they do need to move forward and focus on ways of addressing the harm they caused. Sometimes, there is nothing that the offender can do for his particular victim and community because he may be incarcerated for a crime or may have committed a very violent crime. But there are other things in terms of the greater community that they can do to be both accountable and to try to heal the harm."

"I'm always fascinated and really moved by the reaction from the offenders. It's truly a spiritual experience," Professor Geske, says.

She goes to other prisons as well and says that the victims and survivors that go along with her are committed to the Restorative Justice Programs because they see good coming from the harm done to them or their loved ones. She feels the offender benefits from the experience as well and even if they never leave prison they can change their attitudes, their behavior and reach out to other inmates.

As a passionate supporter of Restorative Justice Professor Geske is often asked to speak on the subject and she is infectious. She draws you in and makes you want to be part of the excitement and hope that Restorative Justice offers.

Tina – Drug Addict
Drug & Alcohol Court

Red Hook
Community Justice Center

Judge Alex Calabrese

"No matter how far a person falls, they can always rise up and overcome the most amazing obstacles if given the right opportunity and support."
Judge Alex Calabrese

Tina's Story
of Drug Addiction

Near dawn, on a cold-wintery morning in February of 2002, Tina, a homeless drug and alcohol addict in Brooklyn, New York was severely beaten. She funded her habit by prostitution. She was paid by her previous evening's client and decided to head back out to the street. On the way, she was robbed and beaten senseless. Her head was bruised and bleeding. She took some money she had hidden in her bra and went to a nearby store and brought a wig to cover up the effects of the beating.

Later in the week she was arrested and taken to Red Hook Community Justice Center in Brooklyn. Tina said, "I was still in a lot of pain from the beating and must have been a sorrowful sight when I appeared before the judge."

Since 1999, she had been living in the Red Hook area and would use the public housing hallways for sleeping and prostitution and was repeatedly arrested for prostitution and trespassing. Since Red Hook had opened their Community Justice Center in April of 2000 when she was arrested she went there. Her many previous arrests has landed her in downtown Brooklyn.

"I guess you could call me a repeat offender which is really an understatement," she said. The first few times she was arrested and taken to Red Hook she received, from her perception, "a slap on the wrist." After she was told to enter drug rehab and do community service, she would promise to do whatever they asked; then would not keep her appointment for detox and would not show up for community service. The basic reason was that once back on the street she would return to her drugs and completely forget about her promises. Because she was not cooperating with the court mandate, a warrant would go out for her arrest and she would get picked up and go back into court. After being arrested several times, the court started to know her face and realized they were seeing a pattern.

However, on that fateful winter day, when Tina stood before Judge Calabrese after having suffered a horrible beating, she felt very defeated and completely worn out. The Judge noted the awful physical condition of the woman standing before him and felt great compassion for her. He noticed how thin and depleted she was and realized she had been coming in and out of his courtroom as though it had a revolving door for the past few months. He checked her complete criminal record and saw that over several years she had been arrested twenty-one times. Most of those arrests were made in downtown Brooklyn, but the latest series of arrests were in Red Hook. With addicts, the Judge always attempted a therapeutic approach, and if they were arrested repeatedly, he let them come in and out of his court room a few more times. So when he cracked down on them he had more leverage. Tina's time had come.

The Judge talked to her gently and started out by complimenting her on her service in the military since he saw on her record that she was a veteran. He then assured her that her criminal record only consisted of civil cases like loitering, prostitution and criminal possession but nothing substantial or very serious like robbery, assault, or breaking and entering. He expressed frustration with the attorneys in the court room, "Why are you thinking of sending this woman to jail?" he asked. Why aren't we getting her some help? There is obviously a problem here. I'm not sending this woman to jail. She needs help!" The Judge started to speak directly to Tina and asked her if she was willing to get herself together and seek treatment for her addiction. He spoke about the realities of living on the street and emphasized, "If you keep this up you are going to be dead."

Tina was so miserable and hurting, that the Judge was starting to get through to her, She started listening to what he was saying. It began to have an impact. She knew her days were numbered because she had already been hospitalized twice for other injuries following beatings. Once she had an infection in her heart valve from shooting heroin with dirty water. Another time she had an infection in her back from giving herself drugs intravenously and was told at the time she might not walk again. Fortunately, she was lucky enough to have recovered from both situations. As the judge spoke, she could feel desperation building up inside her, "Maybe my luck is running out," she thought. "Perhaps I should take the Judge's advice."

As she listened more intently to the Judge, she began to realize he was offering her the help she needed. He told her she could either spend a year in a residential treatment center for drug rehabilitation or spend sixty days in jail. She had been through the "sixty days in jail routine" before. In New York state you only do a portion of the sixty days which meant she could be back on the street getting high again in forty-five days. She reasoned with herself and knew that the addict part of her wanted to take the sixty-day approach. But, the very small part of her mind that was still alive and thinking decided she better take this chance or she just might not have another one. Besides, what sense would it make to go back to the street and get beat up again. She said, "I knew I was tired, sick, hurting and had no way of getting off the street. So I agreed to be mandated to a year in a residential treatment center."

"At this point in my life I really wanted help, but did not know how to go about getting it," she said. "My situation was desperate. I knew if I didn't avail myself of this opportunity I was going to die. It was so cold outside in the winter I was actually surprised that I was still alive. So many nights seemed like they might be my last and I felt that way on many occasions. I was thirty-three years old, after having spent most of my twenties on the street, I needed to do this. Judge Calabrese gave me this chance to change my life and I will be forever grateful."

Tina was indeed lucky to run into Judge Calabrese, who, beginning in the year 2000, was running one of the first drug and alcohol courts in the United States using Restorative Justice practices. At Red Hook the he was able to offer many different approaches to treatment for the addict instead of prison. He believed they were not criminals but sick people in desperate need of treatment for their addiction. However, he did believe that the jail sentence for drug addicts was necessary because that gave him the leverage he needed to get them into drug treatment. Drug and alcohol addicts are surrounded by their victims due to the rippling effect but, they are both victims and offenders to themselves.

Why did Tina Live on the Streets?

How did Tina, a very bright, pretty African American child with a beautiful smile from Brooklyn, New York, become a runaway at thirteen years of age? The answer to that question is all too familiar. Her mother was an alcoholic who was physically and verbally abusive to her during her childhood and her father had disappeared. Her mother's visiting male friends physically and sexually abused Tina, so she had no protection as a child. At thirteen years of age she felt she could not take it any more. She had to leave. There were no family members stable enough for her to turn to for help, so she lived on the streets and often stayed with friends whose parents didn't care what was going on.

She had dropped out of high school and was forced into prostitution to survive. At the age of fifteen, she met a thirty-five year old man who got a room for her and took care of her. She knew he was a bit unstable, but she had little choice in the matter. By the age of sixteen she had gotten her GED and started college, but during this time she had starting using coke and drinking alcohol. Those two addictive elements would eventually become a serious problem for her, but they also served to deaden the pain and loss of a family and a normal childhood.

Around the time she turned eighteen, she decided to enlist in the U.S. Army to get away from the man who was keeping her. "He had become physically abusive to me and acted periodically like a psycho," she said. At first, Tina, liked the service because it gave her an independence and a security she never had. However, it was difficult for her to adjust to all the requirements and responsibilities that it takes to be a soldier. Plus, the military's structure and authority was very uncomfortable for her and she did not handle that well. Tina's lack of responsible role models as a child was a real void in her development and left her unprepared for a career in the military. Also, at this point in her life, the strong urge to bury the pain of her childhood and adolescence in alcohol was becoming more intense.

She just wanted to party and drink alcohol and did that excessively whenever she could. Her military career started in Virginia, she was stationed in Germany for eighteen months and came stateside after that. She came close to completing her four-year tour of duty but toward the end of her enlistment she tested positive, twice, for marijuana. The first time she was given a warning but the second time she was quickly discharged but still given an honorable discharge.

Tina explained, "I was glad to get out of the army and really needed to leave, because I was always putting myself in harm's way." She rejected those who tried to counsel her and work with her. "My captain and first sergeant really liked me and suggested that I stop the alcohol but I was an addictive person and needed the alcohol and wanted the drugs back but couldn't get to them. All the military restrictions made me angry and depressed and all I wanted to do was drink." When she did drink, it would be to excess causing her to black out. She often woke up in places she had no business being. She would then be listed as missing and the army would have to find her, she admitted, "I was a problem soldier."

In 1990 she was discharged and came home to Brooklyn pregnant by a soldier from her platoon and her hometown.

When he was finally able to return to the states they got married. He hoped to stay stateside so she could go back to school and get her degree, but that did not work out because he was sent back overseas. Tina said, "My husband had planned on sending for me and the baby but that never happened. I was able to keep in touch with him for the rest of my pregnancy and for about a year after our son was born. He did send money for our support and I worked at odd jobs during that time. However, after my son was a year old, I never heard from him again and haven't heard from him since.

Tina continued to try to hold down a job when she could. She and her son moved in with an aunt, one of her father's sisters who she had recently connected with. "She didn't charge me rent and I lived with her in Brooklyn," she said.

"Shortly after moving in with her I started drinking heavily again and when my son was three or four months old I was reintroduced to coke. During the week I worked and my aunt took care of my son and on the weekends my mother-in-law would take care of him. On Friday, after taking my son to my mother-in-law's home, I would sit with him for awhile and then sneak out and go on a binge that lasted till Sunday night. On Monday morning, I would pick my son up, take him back to my aunt's and go to work. Sometimes I used coke during the week but mostly just on the weekends. But that routine didn't last long."

Soon she was back using coke and drinking every day and not taking care of her son. After a short time, her aunt and uncle took guardianship of her son. When he was about eighteen-months old, Tina got pregnant again -- the father was someone she had been partying with. She had never used coke when she was pregnant with her son but did during this pregnancy. "However," she said, "Two weeks before my delivery date I stopped using coke so the baby would not be born toxic. Two days after my daughter's birth my aunt stepped in and I turned guardianship over to her. Then I went out and got high."

Tina was devoid of guilt feelings at the time because she said, "I did not feel anything. I was just numb. The drugs and alcohol just blocked all the pain and that was my defense. I would not allow myself to really think about anything except to just stay high. I did feel really bad when visiting my children and that would make me want to get high, even more. While visiting them at my aunts (they stayed with two different aunts) they never told me to stay away and when in my children's presence I did my best not to be high, but I did not see them on a regular basis. My aunts, who were both my father's sisters, did a good job with my children and I was very lucky to have them. Shortly after my daughter was born, I quit working and headed for the streets. I lost all sense of responsibility and used whatever money I had for drugs."

Since leaving the army, Tina's life had taken a complete nose dive. She was now heavily involved with drugs and alcohol and had given up guardianship of her two children. She lived solely on the streets for about the next ten years except for one short relationship with a guy. She sadly added, "I lived in parks, rooftops and hallways -- anywhere I could find. I was a prostitute and not a pretty one. I was a horror."

Tina had begun smoking crack, but soon made the leap to heroin because the cocaine and crack made her nervous and paranoid but the heroin calmed her and made her feel good -- she could zone out for hours on end and not feel anything. "In the beginning, I snorted heroin but soon became an IV user. When that happened, I went back to smoking crack, which is stronger than coke because it contains more chemicals, took pills for anxiety that I bought on the street and continued drinking alcohol." She described her situation by saying she couldn't have one without the other because she would not feel complete. If she had heroin without crack and alcohol, she didn't feel good and needed to have all three. She would get high a little but was taking just enough to keep her physically going because if she took too much she could quickly get into an overdose situation.

She said "I would go to soup kitchens maybe three times a week to get a decent meal, but eating was not a priority, I was very thin, weighing about ninety-five pounds and in an unhealthy state. Money for all the drugs came from prostitution. It was easy to get business as a prostitute and it financed my habit all those years I was on the street. I got arrested many times and assaulted a few times but felt extremely lucky to only have had one sexually transmitted disease, chlamydia, which I was able to easily get treated for,"

Tina got pregnant one more time in 1995 and lived on the streets the whole pregnancy. She said she never considered having an abortion because she was too out of it to think rationally enough to even consider the option. Her baby, born toxic to heroin and crack, was taken from her at the hospital and given up for adoption.

Letters were sent to her giving her an opportunity to reunite with the baby but they were sent to her aunt's home, so Tina didn't see them until two years later. Because she hd not responded to the letters right away, it would be years later that she would be able to verify her second daughter had been adopted.

For the next seven years she lived on the street, Tina went deeper into drugs, her health deteriorated and she was assaulted three times. The fact that she survived is a miracle.

Tina Toughs her Way through Treatment

When Tina left the Red Hook Community Justice Center she was sent to the hospital for detox -- a painful and difficult process. Every part of her body just clenched. She had constant fevers and serious blood pressure problems which meant she had to be constantly monitored. She was in pretty bad shape. She was able to talk but had poor coordination and problems with her equilibrium which prevented her from walking normally; plus, she was very weak. For the first few days of detox she was on methadone to help her withdraw from heroin. That did not help very much since she had been using it on the street and her tolerance level was high However, it did take a little of the edge off. After seven days, she was transferred from the hospital to the residential treatment center, but the pain of detox did not leave her for at least a month.

Tina described her reaction to the treatment center by saying, "I was totally shocked because there were over three hundred women there in all different stages of recovery and in varying states of emotion. It almost seemed like a foreign country to me because everyone seemed to be speaking a different language. They were talking in a therapeutic community jargon which I did not yet understand. As the initial reaction wore off, the patients and staff welcomed me and some of the older residents tried to care for me -- they gave me clothes, showed me around the building and told me what the routine and the group process was like. At the time, I smoked cigarettes because other patients gave them to me and stayed by me if I was frightened."

At the treatment center, Tina was tested for sexually transmitted diseases and came up negative for every one. She said, "I had myself pretty convinced that I had HIV and when they did a series of tests on me for HIV and those tests came back negative I would cry and cry because it was so unbelievable to be that fortunate." She was retested several times later and always came up negative. Each time she cried in relief and gratitude.

After a month was up, she started to feel better and began going to therapy which became extremely emotional for her because she didn't have her drugs to numb the pain. She said, "I started to have all kinds of feelings, images, thoughts, dreams and memories and began thinking about my children and then everything started to unravel before me and swarm around me all at once, and I thought, Oh My God, What Have I Done?'" Almost immediately, she fell apart emotionally and began crying all the time. She was no longer out of it but was completely conscious. It was very tough. Tina was then sent to a psychiatrist and given antidepressants and anti-anxiety medications which she took for about eighteen months to help her cope with these overwhelming feelings.

The depression and crying continued but was compounded by the intense anger that was building up in her. To help her vent her anger she participated in mock group sessions where she would be allowed to take her anger out on an empty chair. Sometimes the chair would be her mom or whoever assaulted or harmed her. She said, "Strangely enough, that helped me so much because I was able to say what I had been holding in for so many years -- even though it was kinda dangerous because I would sometimes throw the chair and cry uncontrollably. This type of therapy really helped me make a breakthrough."

"When I was a small child I was never able to express what was bothering me and I remember crying a lot. Now I was being allowed to speak about my feelings and put all those thoughts, dreams, images and memories into words. I began to remember things that I hadn't before. I remembered being little -- my mother backslapping me and telling me to shut up and throwing me into a closet -- just because I was expressing myself. I learned that was why it was hard for me to recognize my own feelings and to express them to anyone else because my mother beat me when I did that. In therapy I was encouraged to express my feelings and get them all out of my system."

"I was in the treatment program for about three years. Usually, most people are in this program for twelve to eighteen months, but after spending all this time there I got to know a lot of people and I would beg and beg them not to send me back to Brooklyn. I was afraid to go back there because I felt all this treatment would have been in vain. How would I start over? By getting a mediocre job with no place to live and if you don't have much money, you know what you are going to be surrounded by, I just could not go there."

Tina's Life takes a Dramatic Turn

Fortunately for Tina, an opportunity presented itself. The residential treatment center where Tina was staying was run by Phoenix House. (Phoenix House is one of the nation's leading non-profit substance abuse prevention and treatment service organizations.) The building the treatment center was in also contained medical, dental and legal departments. As a resident of the treatment center, she was allowed to apply for a job that paid a small stipend of two or three dollars a week for doing work for the center or other offices in the same building. While job hunting she began to develop a relationship with one of the dental directors from the dental clinic named Dr. Yardley. Dr. Yardley developed a real affection for Tina because she said, "She stood out from the other patients in the treatment center who sometimes appeared like they were going through the motions, but Tina never acted that way, she always seemed committed to her recovery."

One day Tina was having a casual conversation about her past life as an addict with some people who worked in Dr. Yardley's office. She was describing a friend, a transvestite who she'd hang out with on a street corner in Park Slope. When Dr. Yardley heard her say that, her ears perked up, because she had lived in Park Slope and recalled the street corner Tina was describing. She turned and said to Tina in a sorta kidding-like manner, "That wasn't you in that pink wig, was it?" Tina said, "Oh my God, **Yes!**" Tina then told Dr. Yardley she had many different colored wigs and that was her. Dr. Yardley was shocked! She said she had always thought something was familiar about Tina that she could not quite explain. Dr. Yardley suddenly felt really connected to this young woman and had a deep desire to help her. "If you really want help getting a job I will help you," she told Tina. Would you be interested in training to be my assistant if I sent you to school. Tina excitedly responded, "Absolutely!" and that is exactly what happened. Dr, Yardley told her she could stay in Westchester County where the treatment center was located and she would not have to go back to the city. Tina was extactic!

Tina got hands-on-training at the dental clinic and went to school for six months to be trained as a dental assistant. The clinic hired her and rented her a room on another floor of the building where residents from the treatment center were not allowed. She was charged sixty dollars a week for her room and was allowed to stay there for a year until she was able to get her own place. Not until that moment did she really believe she would not have to go back to the city and the streets.

After her training as a dental assistant, she decided she wanted to become a dental hygienist. So she saved enough money to buy a car, enrolled at a nearby college and attended school after work. When she finished her first semester, she finally moved out of the building where the treatment center and dental clinic were located. She rented a co-op in a nice, quiet neighborhood and said, "I'm the only African American in my neighborhood but it is a safe area and no street corner messes are going on."

Tina expects to graduate from college in 2009. She works all day and goes to school three nights a week. Last semester she was able to do most of her classes online. She liked that because it cut down on her winter driving -- she discovered there is a lot of snow north of the city.

She completed the biological science program but then decided not to be a dental hygienist because she would need to go to school full time. "I couldn't do that because I needed to work full time to pay my bills," she said. So she changed her major to business management and hoped to eventually work in human resources.

Her change in her major fit right into the big promotion Dr. Yardley gave her at the dental clinic -- she become the dental coordinator for four different clinics in different areas. The job gave her a lot of responsibility and Tina was so proud and excited to be promoted. She exclaimed, "It was hard to believe that this had really happened to me. I just couldn't believe my good fortune."

Dr. Yardley explained, "When I knew that my coordinator was going to leave there was no question in my mind that Tina was going to get to replace her. She is such a quick learner, intelligent and just about the hardest worker I have ever seen." Dr. Yardley continued and seemed unable to stop the accolades, "She comes in every morning before everyone else and always has everything ready for the day. Beside being thoughtful, considerate, loyal and caring -- she is just about everything you would ever want in an employee and is also one of the nicest people I have ever met."

Tina is obviously very appreciative for the opportunities that have been made available to her and Dr. Yardley is the first person to say that Tina deserves everything she has achieved.

Tina said, "In my promotion at the Dental Clinic I had twelve dental assistants under me that I supervised. Things were going very well for me. But, to my delight and surprise, it got even better. After a few years at that job, I was offered and accepted another job in Human Resources with Phoenix House as a National Training Administrator. They wanted to hire me even before I graduated from college!"

It seems that no one is more suited for that position than Tina. Once on the ladder of opportunity Tina climbed it quickly. I guess she was making up for lost time.

Tina said, "Every day I thank God that I am here and doing this great job! It is just incredible to me, I can hardly believe this is me!"

Tina's Personal Life Needs Love & Mending

Tina is a great example for other addicts and often shares her life's journey with them by volunteering time at Phoenix House where she was treated. She tells the women stories of her past experiences and facilitates workshops and group programs with them. If she can give them an incentive to get clean by letting them know there is a better way of life, then it's time well spent. Her volunteer activity there is always a reminder of her addiction and a validation of what she has been through. She says, "I tell them that I made it and they can too. It's very rewarding for me."

"I have only been out of rehab for a little more than three years so in some ways I am still taking baby steps, and it's important that I do not allow myself to get overwhelmed. That's OK with me because right now my life is going well and I have great friends that are my age. They know my history, respect my past and don't impose alcohol on me when we are together. However, I do admit to feeling far behind when they talk about their high school and college years. At those times, I remind myself how fortunate I am that I got out of a horrible situation and turned my life around."

Tina is still very cautious around alcohol and says that the holidays are sometimes difficult for her. "I'm a regular attendee of Narcotic Anonymous (NA) and during the holidays I stay close to them and attend more meetings than usual because I do not have good memories about Christmas as a child. It was depressing for me when I was little. So the last couple of years I have been trying to change how I celebrate Christmas and make it more enjoyable for me. I treat my-self to all the trimmings and bake special things just for myself. I did not get these things before but I can have them now."

Tina recently discovered that her first husband divorced her in 1999 and she never received the notification. That relieved her of a nag-ging problem and gave her the freedom to marry her fiance, Ulysses. They were married in the fall of 2008. She is very excited about beginning this whole new chapter in her life.

Ulysses is fifty-one years old, holds two jobs, a courier for a lab, and a cook. She met him at the residential treatment center where he has worked for some time. She added, "He is a past drug addict also, so we have that in common and can help each other. Besides, he is my best friend and a great guy. He helps me in so many ways and I feel lucky to have found him. It is such a good feeling when he tells me how proud he is of my accomplishments."

Tina has finally connected with two of her three children. She said, "The first few years I was clean I was afraid to see my children be-cause people did not believe that I could stay clean and really did not trust me. My aunts did not want me jumping in and out of my children's lives but by the third year they began to see me as stable and started to trust me and that felt good.

So she was able to begin a relationship with her son when he was fifteen. He recently enlisted in the Navy and she is so proud of him. Before he joined the Navy, he often visited her on weekends when he was not playing in the New York City Marching Band where he used his exceptional musical talent by playing the sax, horn and piano.

Her second child, a daughter, was on drugs but has recently gone into treatment for mental health issues and drug abuse. Tina is giving her all the support she can and is hoping she will learn from her mother's experience.

Her son knows her story and Tina said, "I gave him a book to read "A Memoir of an Addict" to help him understand me better but so far he has not expressed any feelings about my addiction. We have not broken that barrier yet. However, he is always happy to see me and always wants to be around me. I don't see any anger in him and I thinks he is just glad that I am OK. I am always glad to hear from my daughter and I pray for her all the time. I have not had contact with my adopted daughter but hopefully when she is eighteen I will have that opportunity. I could be rejected, and that of course, would be painful. I always have to be concerned about my emotional health. I went to the residential treatment center in 2002 and got out in 2005. Not that long ago. So I need to proceed very carefully with my personal life and only absorb back into my life what I can handle emotionally."

When Tina mentions Judge Calabrese her eyes sparkle, "I do stay in close touch with him and he has always been there for me. He married Ulysses and I and that was a great honor for me plus he presided over the ceremony where I got my Certificate of Civil Judgment which means that all my arrest cases are closed now. If I had to look for another job my arrest record won't be a problem."

I often give him a call and tell him how I'm doing and send him cards and letters on Christmas and on other occasions. He is truly a wonderful man and really responsible for changing my life. When I graduated from the residential center he came to my graduation and told me, 'I wouldn't have missed this for the world' and he promises to be at my college graduation. He will always be part of my life as I go through certain landmarks that I want to share with him. He is very important to me and I have so much love and respect for him because of what he did for me and what he continues to do for others."

Epilogue

Tina has shown tremendous courage in telling her story because of her strong desire to help others who are addicts and to give back to her community.

It is hard to imagine her childhood with the abuse she suffered; physical, mental and sexual along with the obvious neglect of her emotional needs as a growing child. She knew she had to run away, but it was unfortunate there was no place to run to besides the street. It's difficult to imagine the hardships of living on the streets for so many years, in all kinds of weather, with no place to call home and no one who really cares about you.

Alcohol and drug addiction has become an increasing problem in the United States and is one of the leading causes of death among young adults. More than fifty percent of all auto accidents involve drugs or alcohol and a large percentage of prisoners in our country's prisons are suffering from addiction. These people are often not criminals and should be in treatment at an appropriate facility for their disease, not in prison. Millions of tax dollars and millions of lives could be saved, as Tina's was, if we face this problem head on. We need to open up more Drug and Alcohol Courts and use Red Hook as a model.

"Drug addiction is a chronic relapsing brain disease characterized by compulsive drug seeking and use despite often devastating consequences," said Dr. Nora Volkow, Director of the National Institute on Drug Abuse from the National Institutes of Health. "It results from a complex interplay of biological vulnerability, environmental exposure, and developmental factors, for example, the addict's stage of brain maturity. Scientists estimate that genetic factors account for forty to sixty percent of an individual's vulnerability to addiction, with environmental and developmental variables influencing whether and how particular genes are expressed. "

As we saw with Tina, addiction ruins capable and intelligent human beings. She did recover, but the devastation to her life was catastrophic and she will be dealing with the aftermath for the rest of her life.

This disease needs treatment like all other diseases and we, as a society, need to address the problem and treat the disease not criminalize the patient. Tina was indeed fortunate to be at the right place at the right time -- the Drug and Alcohol Court at the Red Hook Community Justice Center before Judge Alex Calabrese. Judge Calabrese, having vast experience with addicts, knew just how to deal with her situation and was able to choose the most opportune time to convince her to take the treatment option. Otherwise, she could have died or been imprisoned and continued through the revolving prison door. This approach wastes contributing members of our society to addiction.

We need to forcibly address the issue and get Drug and Alcohol Courts in our communities to save the lives of our family members, our neighbors and members of our community. The Red Hook Community Justice Center, at the time of Tina's arrest, was only the second Community Justice Center in the nation. The first was in midtown Manhattan. Red Hook has had many successes like Tina's.

Restorative Justice – Healing & Redemption

The Red Community Justice Center is unique because it recognizes that neighborhood problems do not always conform to the arbitrary jurisdictional boundaries of the modern court system. Because Red Hook is multijurisdictional, the boundaries are flexible and do not inhibit family cases and drug cases to overlap in terms of problem solving. That is one of the secrets of its success.

Judge Calabrese spends much of his very limited free time talking to guests from all over the nation and the around the globe who are trying to replicate what he has accomplished. Many of our states and some countries are running out of jail space and have overwhelming substance abuse problems. Red Hook has become not only a model for our nation but also a model for the world.

Section IV tells the story of how Red Hook was established and how it functions to give people back their lives as well as their community

Section II

✳

International Restorative Justice

Criminal Justice & Peacemaking

New Zealand's Restorative Justice System

The "Most" Restorsative Justice System in the World

*says, Allan MacRae, Youth Justice Practice Advisor
for the South Island of New Zealand*

*Forgiveness is not forgetting
or foregoing Justice.*

New Zealand

"The <u>Most</u> Restorative Justice System In The World"

In the 1980s, New Zealand's criminal justice system was in crisis. Its indigenous-tribal people, the Maoris, made up a large percentage of New Zealand's prison population even though they were a minority. Their welfare system was overwhelmed. The Maoris wanted change. They asked their government to stop its institutional racist policies and to stop imprisoning their troubled youth. They requested that the crime problem be addressed in an appropriate forum, turned over to their tribes, their families and extended families.

The Maori had a commitment to their children to make things right if their children did something wrong and hurt someone. They wanted a voice in addressing the crime problem and to use the resources of their extended family and the community at large. They believed they could handle the problems of their youth themselves by using their culture's traditional decision-making processes which included the principles and values that had guided their people for many generations. These principles would later become known as Restorative Justice.

The New Zealand government listened to the Maori people and in 1989 the legislature passed a landmark Act of Parliament called

Restorative Justice – Healing & Redemption

"The Children, Young Persons and Their Family Act." The corner-stone of this Act is Family Group Conferences (FGC). These conferences have changed their juvenile justice system and reduced juvenile crime. Today, New Zealand has the "Most Restorative Justice System in the World.

Family Group Conferences usually include the victim, the victim's extended family, the offender, the offender's extended family, a police officer, a FGC Coordinator and others who may be appropriate.

The Act mandates that when a young person is involved in serious criminal behavior the extended family is entitled to become immediately involved. Then, based on the Act's goals and principles, the family is required to be consulted on the process the Family Group Conference will follow. The police cannot bring charges into Court unless those charges have met the requirements set forth in the Act that allows arrest. In all other circumstances, a Family Group Conference is held to determine if the young person should be prosecuted.

When it is decided that a young person needs to be charged, the young person is asked if they deny or do not deny the charge. If the matter is not denied the Judge is required to direct a Family Group Conference to convene. If there is criminal accountability, then another Family Group Conference needs to be convened to recommend what form restitution and punishment will take.

An example of how a court-directed Family Group Conference would work follows in a brief true story of a young fourteen-year old boy who committed a very serious crime -- the rape of a three-year old girl. When his Family Group Conference convened it was discovered by the offender's family that significant influences and behaviors surrounding the offender were happening at the time of the rape. The victim's family was informed of these circumstances. Then the little girl's family told the offender's family about the pain and anguish they had suffered because of this horrible offence to their little daughter. The offender's family listened intently to what was said because the opinion of the parents of this little girl needed to take precedence in deciding the offender's fate.

The young offender and his family needed to agree to try to do what the little girl's family required. They had to address the effect of the crime on the victim and the family. Also they needed to take steps to prevent it from happening again by addressing the underlying causes. The offender's family met alone as a group and agreed to do everything within their power to satisfy the victim's needs.

The Family Group Conference reconvened with both families and through discussion and negotiation reached a consensus together about how they wanted to see this young man punished. They also decided on the method of restitution and what form that would take. This was followed by a formal agreement between the families outlining the consequences to the young boy for his crime. Then the agreement was turned over to professionals to carry out the punishment and restitution.

The victim's parents and family needed to know that the young man fully understood the effect he had on them and the effect on their little girl as she grew up. They did not want this to ever happen to another child and their family.

Through the confidentiality process of the Family Group Conference, they were given the information required to make informed decisions and agreed on a plan that held the young person accountable and had the greatest chance to prevent further offending. For the victim and their family to reach this point there is usually acceptance and maybe even an underlying feeling of forgiveness occurring in the conference, allowing the healing to begin.

This particular young person was allowed to stay out of jail but was given extensive counseling, constant supervision and was put under the care and protection of the Department of Social Welfare until he was nineteen years of age. The offender's family was responsible for all the tenets of this mandate to be carried out. This decision gave this young man a significant opportunity to turn his life around, whereas, if he had gone to jail he probably would have served five years and had very little treatment. The emphasis in Family Group Conferencing is not just to keep the young person out of jail but to do what is necessary to help ensure that the offender will not re-offend. The offenders are also provided with the opportunities to develop the skills and behaviors that will help them live successfully within the community, rather than those required to survive in jail and within a gang. To assist the conference, health, education and welfare assessments can be requested and are required by police in some circumstances.

This Restorative Justice process that New Zealand uses is different than a victim/offender dialogue. The Family Group Conference is a group-decision-making process that looks at the young person's life in a holistic manner. It recommends to the court whether a young person should be prosecuted and what the young person's restitution should be to the victim.

Allan MacRae, Youth Justice Practice Advisor for the Southern Island region of New Zealand says, "Both addressing the impact on the victim and addressing the underlying causes of the offense is why we have Family Group Conferences. One of the greatest benefits of a group is that the young offender is not alone but supported by a family group and this provides many resources for him. It is also a great benefit for the community. It always amazes me what both victim and offender family groups can do together for the victim. The potential to put things right is multiplied when we can use the resources of the family and not leave it up to just one individual. If the young person was put in jail, there would be no emphasis on helping his victim.

In many of these Conferences the family groups on both sides often come together to help the victim in every way they can and it then becomes a community or tribal effort. It is a 'win win' situation."

MacRae adds, "When I reflect on the Family Group Conferences I have facilitated I am filled with emotion. These feelings come from the suffering I have witnessed but, more importantly, from the powerful processes of healing and forgiveness that I have seen take place."

The Maori

The Maori population of New Zealand are olive complexioned and recognizable as a separate race of people but do not live as a separate people because they are well dispersed among the general population of New Zealand and have been since World War II. They participated in the War because they wanted to be recognized as proud citizens of New Zealand. When colonization began they proved to be a very advanced people and were quick to adapt to European technology.

MacRae adds insight, "Although the Maori are scattered and distributed among our communities they are a minority group. When you have a minority group in your country and the youth of that group only sees people of the majority acknowledged as successful then these youth can become detached from their own traditional support systems and values. They become a subculture and see themselves as unwanted and isolated from their community. We needed to recognize the racial conditions in our country and acknowledge the culture, language and values of the Maori people."

"Once we did this, then the Maori were empowered to address the issues facing their youth. The Act mandated in 1989 gave rights to the parents and extended family of the Maori people and all New Zealand families. Those rights allowed families to be involved at the onset of a criminal charge against their children and then gave them an opportunity to find a resolution amongst themselves by using the goals and principles of the Family Group Conferences. One goal is to reach a consensus between victims and offenders in the resolution to the crime. That, in itself, is remarkable and incredibly restorative."

MacRae points out, "Today, Maoris are our neighbors. Many have very senior professional positions, intermarriage is common and they are fully integrated into our communities. We work together and play together as one people. However, the Maori people do need to maintain their cultural values and tribal connections -- it is part of their identity. There are many different tribes and they often have tribal conferences and operate businesses under tribal auspices. At the same time, they may own personal businesses."

The tribes have traditions that have been passed down through families for generations and one of those traditions is the basic tenet of Restorative Justice: When a tribal member does harm to another that harm must be made right for the injured person and the whole tribe becomes involved to make that happen. This tradition has certainly been to the benefit of all New Zealanders and perhaps the world.

"Children, Young Persons & their Family" Act

MacRae says, "No one else in the world is doing Restorative Justice as New Zealand does it. No one has it legislated as we do and no one else mandates that if a young person is arrested almost immediately he/she and their family has a FGC Coordinator assigned to them and must have a Family Group Conference before the court can impose a sentence."

The requirements for arresting young persons are: for giving false information to the police, if they are likely to re-offend in the time before their case can be dealt with or if they are likely to not show up at court. If a young person does not meet the requirements for arrest, the Police must refer the young person to a FGC Coordinator for a Family Group Conference to be held before they can bring charges to the Court. There are very tight times frames for this to occur. A court-directed Family Group Conference must be convened within fourteen days and the conference must be completed in an additional seven days.

During those fourteen days that young person cannot be sent to prison but must be placed with caregivers. However, if the public interest requires it, the young person can be placed in the custody of the Chief Executive of the Ministry of Social Development who has the discretion to place that young person in the community or in one of New Zealand's purpose-built residences. Individual circumstances are taken into consideration. This all applies to young people under seventeen years of age at the time they committed an offence.

The court refers all very serious charges to Family Group Conferences with the exception of murder or manslaughter charges. Murder has a mandatory life sentence in New Zealand.

Every other serious charge against a young person, including rape, arson, aggravated robbery, attempted murder or wounding with intent to cause bodily harm goes to Family Group Conferencing. If the young person is seventeen or younger they will not go to jail unless the Court has explored all other alternatives available.

At a Family Group Conference, the offender's family members are asked right from the beginning how they are going to take care of the victim's needs because that is paramount. Then they are asked how they are going to run their conference. It is all about the family having ownership of the process, which in turn gives them ownership of the decisions. This way of proceeding gives the family greater motivation to see that all the issues are dealt with and completed.

Family Group Conferences are designed for the top twenty percent of offenders involved in a serious crime. Out of this, sixty percent of cases have one Conference and the offenders are not seen again. Twenty percent have only two Conferences. Based on this information, New Zealand officials know that they need to put their energy and effort into the remaining twenty percent, as they are the most likely to become recidivist or lifestyle offenders.

MacRae makes an interesting observation, "Some young people who offend do not have family available to support them in their Family Group Conference, but the family does not have to be blood family but can be a group of people looking out for the interest of the young offender. We have actually created families around young people by empowering the community to become involved. The young person can be very isolated and have no sense of belonging. Interventions aimed at giving them back connections with good adult role models, such as leaders within their extended family and culture, lead to lifetime changes. Statistics show that the majority of young offenders who follow through with their plans from their Family Group Conference never offend again during their youth or as adults. In other words, most of those young people choose to stop offending for the rest of their lives. The support created in the Family Group Conference will often stay with that young person long past the formal involvement of the state."

The whole youth justice system in New Zealand is guided by a set of principles. One of the principles is that a young person should not be prosecuted unless it is in the public interest. The police have to qualify why an arrest and charge would be in the public interest and get families involved immediately.

For lower level crimes in New Zealand a person can be arrested and then the police can actually unarrest that person depending on circumstances. Sixty to eighty percent of young people are diverted by the police from formal charges. Then a range of things can happen from a warning, a caution or the police can put a plan together to put things right with their victim -- whatever makes a good outcome.

"For adults we have a whole different range of Restorative Justice processes that vary from Family Group Conference to Community Conference Panels," says MacRae.

"We are having tremendous success, even though the program has been under pressure financially. After the Act came into effect there was a dramatic drop in crime. Before that we had a welfare model and were incarcerating young people at a huge rate believing it was in their best interests. Those young people were not released back into the community until it was felt they had adjusted enough to be allowed to return. This often led to them being incarcerated for a term totally disproportionate to their offence. Now, young people are held accountable in a way that is proportionate to their offending and gives due consideration to the interests of the victim. We now have a balance between a justice model and a welfare model and are capturing the best points from each."

The "Most Restorative Justice System in the World" has attracted interested researchers and observers from many countries including Belgium, Germany, Australia, England, Singapore, Thailand, Israel, Canada, Northern and Southern Ireland and many states in the U. S. All trying to replicate the success of the New Zealand model.

Epilogue

New Zealand's story of Restorative Justice is truly amazing because it has the most restorative justice system in the world. Their system is based on the history of indegenious people's basic values and principles, the most basic being that whenever anyone was harmed in their tribe by another, the tribal community required that restitution be made for the harm done to the victim and the community at large.

This simplistic truth is expressed over and over in this book. We see that it works by healing, changing and transforming lives. However, in today's world, it can sometime seem countercultural to the way we currently operate our criminal justice system with almost no emphasis on the victim and a denial that most offenders will be returning to the commuity. There is no balance in the system and no way to achieve one.

New Zealanders have proven success and can teach us all profound lessons of healing and trnsformation through the Family Group Conferences. The most dramatic lesson of all is if there is not a family available **they make one** by drawing on the community at large to participate and support a young person who has no one to care about them. Then they build a family group around that person to give guidance, direction and emotional support, but the most important element is the commitment to that young person's life to try to get he/she on the right path. They've proven, it works!

On the next page are the goals and principles that New Zealand's Restorative Justice system uses.

Restorative Justice – Healing & Redemption

New Zealand's Restorative Justice System
Goals and Principles for Youth
Between 14 & 17 Years of Age
Who Commit Criminal Acts

Goals
Diversion into the Restorative Justice system that includes FGCs
Victim and family involvement
Accountability by the offender
Consensus decision making
Cultural appropriateness
Due process

Principles
Consider the victim's interests
Avoid criminal proceedings unless
the public interest requires otherwise
Take age into account
Keep offenders in their community -- this prevents isolation
Don't use justice for asssistance programs such as welfare
Strengthen families
The least restrictive option should be promoted
to keep the young person in their family group

"The Little Book of Family Group Conferences" by Howard Zehr and Allan MacRae explains New Zealand's RJ Program in much greater detail. The information for New Zealand's Restorative Justice story is from that book and an interview with Allan MacRae.

International Peacemaking
Restorative Justice Circles

Jews & Palestinians

True peace is not simply the absence of hostilities
or agreements to end violence.
True peace requires a change of heart,
openness to understanding
the life context and suffering
of the other, a willingness to see
the humanity in one's adversary.
Politicians can end the violence
through peace agreements and disarmaments.
Only former enemies and combatants
can build peace within their communities
through human encounter.

Dr. Mark Umbreit

Restorative Justice Circles Palestinians & Jews

Dr. Umbreit said he never thought he would be alive to witness Restorative Justice developing all over the world. He has recently returned from China, Ireland and Israel where he witnessed Restorative Justice Practices being implemented. It is now moving in many directions and way beyond criminal justice.

For example: Dr. Umbreit has been trying to get communities of Jews and Palestinians together in Restorative Justice Circles to promote better understanding between them. He has accomplished this with gatherings in his own living room in his hometown of Minneapolis, Minnesota and in Milwaukee Wisconsin and continues to promote them across the country and around the world.

By using the circle process each person is encouraged to speak and share their narrative while the rest of the circle listens. He emphasizes the need for respect for each person in the circle and the need for everyone to feel safe. Despite one's best efforts, he says "Sometimes it can get quite messy." He has discovered that it is particularly hard, even for the most progressive Jews and Rabbis, to hear narratives from the Palestine perspective.

Dr. Umbreit said, "This all sounds bigger that it really is but it does give off little glimmers of hope," he says. "It is not going to solve the world's problems, but in the long term, I believe it contributes to the energy of healing within the global community. I am well aware that what I am doing is only a little drop in the ocean and will initiate only a few ripples, but I also know anytime people who hate one another or what the other represents and if they can sit in a room and listen to each other in a respectful way with no expectations of agreeing -- somehow this experience has tremendous impact on people's lives and creates a powerful dynamic that often can move toward understanding and healing. I have witnessed it and seen it happen."

Restorative Justice Circles, Milwaukee WI

The Restorative Justice Circles that took place in Milwaukee between the Palestinian and Jewish communities had two knowledgeable and interesting participants: Rakefet Ginsberg an Israeli emissary to the Milwaukee Jewish Foundation; and Othman Atta, an attorney and Palestinian from the Arab community in Milwaukee. The circles met a few times and were facilitated by Professor Janine Geske and Dr. Mark Umbreit. There were several representatives from the local Palestinian and Israeli communities: four Palestinians including Othman who was born in the West Bank; three Jews including Rakefet who was born in Israel and the assistant district attorney in Milwaukee. At their first gathering they had two guests, an Israeli woman and a Palestinian man who were on a speaking tour with families of people who were killed in the Palestinian/Israeli conflict. This human connection via the Restorative Justice Circle was very important to all of the participants and they were eager to express their viewpoints about their homelands.

In the following commentary Othman and Rakefet give their reflections on their experience in Restorative Justice Circles.

Rakefet Ginsberg was a soldier in the Israeli military for two years and then a social worker in the army for six years. She has been living in the United States for the past two years with her family and will return to Israel in August of 2009. She is employed by the Milwaukee Jewish Federation as an Israeli Emissary and as director of the Israel Center which strengthens links between Milwaukee and Israel through various types of programming. *(Please note that the opinions expressed here are the personal thoughts of Rakefet Ginsberg and do not reflect the point of view of the Milwaukee Jewish Foundation.)*

Rakefet has participated in two types of Restorative Justice Circles. The first was held in Turkey with sixteen professional women -- eight Israeli women and eight Palestinian women who were specifically selected to attend this event. They spent four days together and three or four months later met again in Israel for four more days.

She said, "After being selected to participate in this Restorative Justice Circle and before leaving for Turkey, I began to develop fearful thoughts because I would be meeting with Palestinian women. I was not sleeping well and found myself dreaming that in the airport one of the Palestinian women opened her coat, exposed a bomb and blew us all up. It was a surprise to me to learn that I possessed that kind of fear."

"On the first day of the circle, the Palestinian women seemed united in their thoughts. I don't think they felt safe enough to express different opinions," Rakefet said. "The Israeli women were the exact opposite and were comfortable voicing various points of view because we live in a democratic society and we're not afraid to dialogue inside and outside of our government. In Israel, it is all right to disagree with something our government does and still agree with basic Israeli principles. The Palestinian women seemed rather reticent to share an individual opinion. After four days, however, they began to be open up and said there are different versions of the facts and on specific points they strongly disagreed with us, but this type of dialogue was very hard for them to participate in; it made them uneasy."

Rakefet continued, "I must say that those fours days were one of the most powerful adventures I had ever had, and I had come to this situation after eight years in the Israeli army and also felt very self-assured that I knew what was right and what was wrong. I ended up with great empathy for these women. For the first time, I heard the Palestinian side of the story, not the media story and not how the Palestinian leaders wanted it to be presented. This experience changed my viewpoint, not my political viewpoint, but it changed the way I understood the situation and helped me to fully realize how incredibly complicated the situation really is."

"When we were sitting in the circle together we spent a lot of time listening to one another and always gave the person speaking our respect. There was an acknowledgement that each side was hurting the other and this helped me to develop a deeper understanding for their situation," she said. "Amazingly, we discovered that we did see many things in a similar manner. Sometimes there was even laughter and it was clear that we shared many cultural aspects in common. We ate similar food, enjoyed similar music and even the Jewish and Muslim religions shared similarities and holy places. Essentially, the circle helped me to understand myself better and to see the Palestinians in a different light."

"However, when returning home to Israel I had to face the reality of the incredible complexity of the Palestinian/Israel conflict, but, I must admit, I did have a bit more confidence that we would find a way to solve it."

"Four months later, when we met again -- inside Israel this time -- the experience was different. It was more like being on the third side of the issue and it seemed to be tension-filled. To meet with us, the Palestinian women came to Israel from the West Bank and needed to go through the usual checkpoints so this created a more negative emotional atmosphere than our previous meeting. At that meeting, we were in a neutral setting, it went smoother and was more comfortable.

In our discussions, the second time, I found myself in disagreement with some of the Jewish women who were present. They were very extreme in their viewpoints and said our problems can be solved 'if we do this and you do that.' No two-step solution will solve anything in this situation -- it is more likely that two hundred steps will be needed," Rakefet said.

For Rakefet, it was positive to have respectful discussions with Palestinians because in Israel she does not meet many Palestinians on a daily basis. And, if she does have an encounter with them, it is always filled with tension. This, of course, is a big part of their problem. They are close physically but are separated by their ideology.

Rakefet continued, "The Milwaukee Restorative Circle that I attended became a bit argumentative and we did not share our stories as openly and freely as I had in the previous circles in Turkey and Israel," she said. "I think the makeup of the circle did not help. Some attendees had lived in Israel or Palestine; others had only visited these countries. It really makes a difference to actually live in the country that you represent, otherwise, I feel you don't understand the dynamics that the people living there are faced with. It was hard to relate to the people who had only been in Israel temporarily because they were really speaking from general knowledge. They certainly care about Israel, but for me, Israel is my life and it is part of my past, present and future. I was born in Israel, so were my parents and my grandparents. My mother's family came from Iran in the beginning of the 20th century before Israel even became a state. The reality is that every day I feel the joy and the fear of being an Israeli."

"Personally, I really don't think the Restorative Justice Circles will solve the Israeli/Palestinian problem in a logical way that would lead to a positive conclusion. However, I do think that what came out of this experience was more of an emotional healing on a one-to-one basis and perhaps that's how we will eventually learn to trust one another. It was certainly important to do and I am glad I was able to participate in the Restorative Justice movement. These types of experiences can only lead to a better understanding of each other."

Othman Atta, a naturalized American citizen of Palestinian origin, was born in the West Bank near Jerusalem. Othman is well-known in the Milwaukee area for his civic leadership and is president of the Islamic Society of Milwaukee. He was named Libertarian of the Year in 2002 and he received the "Leaders in Law" award from the Wisconsin Law Journal. Othman spoke about the Restorative Justice Circles held in Milwaukee.

Othman said, "Everyone in the Milwaukee circles were willing to be up front with their opinions and we had many good discussions and when everyone participated we all benefitted. All members of the circles seemed to instantly realize that this type of engagement, with others whose opinion is so opposite to yours, is important because despite our differences, we at least were having a dialogue. When that happens it is much more difficult to pigeon-hole, stereotype or dehumanize another -- especially if the other is representative of a faction that you are alienated by."

Dr. Umbreit, acting as a facilitator, insisted that all members of the circle tell their stories without being interrupted by anyone before they were finished. So people told their individual stories the way they wanted to and no one made any kind of judgment. Othman, said, "I thought this approach was good because most of us didn't know the stories of other individuals in the circle. One of the Palestinians became very emotional when he talked about what his father told him about his land being taken away from him. I knew this man but I never knew this part of his story. He had a big poster with the deed to his family's land."

"On the Jewish side, two people who had actually lived in Israel told their stories and they were extremely interesting to me. They stated their fears and concerns. The other Jewish individuals seem to agree that when they visited Israel everything was wonderful. So, because they had not actually lived in Israel their story was not as meaningful or credible to me."

"I spoke about my grandfather who came to the United States from Palestine in the 1950s. His son -- my dad -- came with my grandfather to finish high school here. While in the United States my grandfather passed away but my father stayed on to finish school and then was drafted into the military reserve for two years, Eventually, he was honorably discharged and ultimately left to return to the West Bank where he married my mother and started a family. In the 1960s he returned to the United States with his family. I was a baby at the time. We entered this country with a large influx of other Palestinians who were emigrating at the same time."

"Our Restorative Justice Circle has not met again for some time and I feel we really need to continue meeting. I hope we can come to some understanding or agreement why we did not previously accomplish more and how we can move on from where we left off. Our gatherings were certainly worthwhile and I look forward to their continuance."

Othman Atta & Rakefet Ginsberg
Solutions
Israeli/Palestinian Conflict

After Othman and Rakefet discussed their experiences of participating in Restorative Circles they gave their thoughts and opinions on possible solutions to the Palestinian/Israeli conflict. They do agree on some issues.

The Restorative Justice movement is hard at work in Israel and the Palestinian territories, and perhaps it will be able to assist in the peace process by promoting better understanding at the grass roots level between these divided people.

The following commentary is presented as an example of an outcome of international efforts with Restorative Justice Practices.

Othman Atta's Solution for Peace in Israel

"Ideally, in my opinion, the solution for peace between the Israelis and the Palestinians is that Israel should become one state," says Othman. This would give every person one vote -- even the Palestinians who were forced to flee. I believe most issues plaguing the peace talks could be resolved with the one-state solution. However, this solution is absolutely rejected by almost every Israeli, including one we were meeting with in the Restorative Justice Circle. There is a small minority of Israelis who advocate for the one-state solution, but in my view, the reason that it does not get support from the rest of the Israeli population is that the birth rate for Palestinians is much higher than it is for Jews and this circumstance alone would not allow the Jews to preserve a Jewish state.

"I can certainly make the one-state argument, but as a Palestinian whose country was destroyed to create the Jewish state, it is really not that acceptable. The other solution is that the West Bank and Gaza become the Palestinian state. That represents about twenty two percent of original Palestine and to have that twenty-two percent become the Palestinian state would mean that seventy-eight percent would remain in the Jewish state. However, I would say that right now, I would be forced to accept this solution. Palestine's current government and many countries in the Arab League have told the Israelis that if they totally evacuate what they occupied in 1967 -- which is the West Bank and Gaza -- the twenty two percent -- then there would be a peace settlement."

"Unfortunately the Israelis say, 'We don't want to give back Jerusalem and some of the settlements that we have built in the West Bank.' So they will not agree to give back the full twenty-two percent to the Palestinians and give up control of Jerusalem."

According to Othman, those settlements are against international law and that is why the Palestinians have created groups like Hamas. Hamas' reaction to the Israeli stance is, "O.K. you don't want to make a deal and don't want to give twenty-two percent back to us, fine, then we will just keep fighting it out until a victor emerges and you will never have peace."

"So, obviously the situation just continues to degenerate," Othman says.

"Younger Jews who weren't involved in the creation of Israel, in many cases, see things in a different light," says Othman. "They make up many different groups, some very religious, indoctrinated settlers, and others who believe God gave them the land of Israel and it belongs to them even though the Palestinians lived on it."

"Also, you have many secular Jews who are involved in advocating for Palestinian rights but they may not necessarily believe in one state."

Othman says, "The Jewish side of the argument is: Look want happened to us historically, the continual persecution and oppression; we need to have our own state and it needs to be a Jewish state." He added, "I disagree with that completely. President Bush, at the sixtieth anniversary of Israel being made an independent state, made a remark that Israel should remain a Jewish state. What kind of equality is that."

According to Othman, the United States has been the biggest challenge to the rationale behind creating the state of Israel, the rationale being: Jews could never be accepted in any society because they would always be discriminated against and there would always be some kind of oppression.

There are more Jews in the United States than there are in Israel and what the Jews have been able to accomplish in the United States has actually proven that premise wrong.

The whole idea of Zionism is that Jews should be able to return to what they consider to be their homeland. United States Jews, by in large, are not doing that, because they are comfortable where they are. Even other Jews who have traveled to Israel from the former Soviet Union ultimately have chosen to leave there and go to the United States.

"One of the problems with American Jews is that you can find very liberal aggressive Jewish individuals who are in the forefront of civil liberties, but when it comes to Israel they are one hundred and eighty degrees on the opposite side. To me, as a Palestinian, this is very painful and very frustrating," Othman says.

When Othman is asked, "What is the solution to the Israeli/Palestinian problem?" Othman says, "Everyone knows what is agreeable to most, including the Israeli population. Return the West Bank and Gaza to the Palestinians. I would say to the Israelis, 'Give ninety-five to ninety-seven percent of the West Bank and Gaza back to the Palestinians.' Set up security for both sides, forget about the unresolved issues for the time being and build the Palestinian society for five years. Pull down the Israeli settlements and get the Palestinians out from under the Israeli military rule. Build up the country and invest money in their society. That will give the Palestinians something to live for. Something to call their own."

"Communication and negotiations should continue with the Israelis. As long as the Israelis are no longer occupiers and no longer controlling their lives, then little by little, some of the Palestinians's rights can be restored. At that point, they can deal with the other issues like Jerusalem." Othman stated, "These are my personal thoughts and feelings."

Regarding Jerusalem, Othman said he believes it should be an open city for all three faiths: Jewish, Christian and Muslim. There are important places of worship for all three faiths in Jerusalem and they should be made accessible to people of each specific faith.

Or, he suggested, use a mixed municipality concept. Israel has controlled Jerusalem since 1948. In Arab East Jerusalem there is a major Muslim mosque and the a well-known Christian place of worship called "The Church of the Holy Sepulchre." So far the Israeli government has been adamant that they want to keep control of the land and the Muslims and the Christians can control what is on the land. He concluded, "I don't think that will work."

Othman - Refugee & Resource Problem

For many years after World War I and after the Ottoman Empire was defeated, the Europeans created countries with artificial borders. There was Palestine, Jordan and Lebanon which were all part of greater Syria. The region along the coast of the Mediterranean Sea was called Palestine but did not have firmly delineated borders. That happened later on. There was no Israel.

"In 1948 the state of Israel was created and in a short period of time about 750,000 Palestinians were made refugees." Othman said. "This is the most contentious issue between Israelis and Palestinians. We have Palestinian refugees in Jordan, Lebanon, Egypt, and the United States and 750,000 has mushroomed into millions. A good guess would be that now there are five million refugees -- I certainly don't think they are all going to return to a Palestinian state. Many would like compensation for their losses and choose to live in the country they are currently living in. For example: I am a refugee and a United States citizen living comfortably. Would I go back? Most likely not, and neither will my children. Maybe the refugee in Lebanon who is offered Lebanese citizenship, or citizenship in another country may take that opportunity. Only some Palestinians would return. This could certainly be worked out."

"Furthermore, according to international law, people who were forced to flee or fled have a right to return to their homes. That seems to apply to the whole world -- except to the Palestinians. The Israeli government and their supporters say we could never allow that, because if we allowed the Palestinians to return, Jews will become a minority. So we wind up back at square one, which is the main issue, that Jews will be outnumbered and unable to remain a Jewish state so that they can protect themselves."

Othman says, "Take someone who is Jewish who never had any family ties or connection to the land of Israel. They get off the plane there and demand Israeli citizenship and they get it. Those who had property there, a history there, roots there, but for the simple fact that they are not Jewish they are not allowed citizenship. The injustice of it all."

"For example, after Saddam was toppled, Chili was the only country that would take the Palestinians living in Iraq. Israel would not take them back and neither would many of the Arab countries. Blame is shared with the Israeli-Jewish community and the Arab countries who are governed by autocratic dictator regimes that want to preserve themselves. The Palestinian issue continues to fester all over the Mideast."

According to Othman, there is a severe water problem in the Mideast. Major aquifers under the West Bank supply water to the whole surrounding area. This is of great concern to the Israelis and adds to the problem of giving up the West Bank to the Palestinians because the Israelis want to keep control of the water. An agreement will need to be made for water usage. In the north, water sources are available but control of the water is creating a difficult situation. Unless leaders are willing to sit down and come up with a solution that is fair and reasonable then a water crisis is on the horizon. This crisis cannot be solved by one country -- all Mideast countries must work together. Othman doesn't see that happening.

One could sense Othman's discouragement when he said, "I try to be an optimist but it is hard. My immediate family and I have nothing to worry about but I can't just forget about the Palestinian problem. It is part of my heritage and part of me because I have family and friends in the West Bank. My own mother and father came from the West Bank. It is very emotional for me. Many people that I know have suffered a terrible injustice. Circumstance gave me this great life in America but I have a responsibility to others left in this deplorable situation."

Rakefet's Solution for Peace in Israel

"The one-state solution will not work," Rakefet says. "I am not living in Israel just because it is a nice place to live, but because it is a Jewish democratic state. I cannot give up either one of them -- the democratic part or the Jewish part. Which means if I want it to stay democratic and a million and a half Palestinian refugees become Israeli citizens, then, fifteen or twenty years from now, Israel will no longer be a Jewish state anymore. Only democratic. I can't have both -- I want to have both because that is what Israel is all about."

"I'm not sure that there are any Jews that think there shouldn't be a Jewish state because of the huge need within the Jewish soul. It is not a reality to think that three million Arabs living inside of Israel will let it remain a Jewish state if the Jews are not in the majority."

"The reason I feel so strongly about this is because for the last 2000 years the Jews have been persecuted throughout the world. Many of my friends arrived in Israel after running away from other places in the world where they were minorities and where they were persecuted. Jews came to Israel even before it was a state because it was the only place where they felt like they belonged and felt safe. Every country around us wants to get rid of us -- that's a great argument for the Jewish state."

Rakefet, along with her entire family, is, has been, or will be in the Israeli army. That includes her husband, her brother, her father who was wounded in war -- and someday her three sons. She has known many people who have died defending Israel.

She said, "Meeting with the Palestinian women was hard, and I never cried so much for myself, for them and for the reality that we face. The Palestinian women were from Nablus and they kept telling us not to support the Israeli army. I remember saying to them, 'What do you mean?' My son is fourteen and in four years he is going to go into the army. Of course, I don't want my son in the army but what choice do I have I want him to stay in Israel and protect the Jewish state so my grandchildren can have a safe place to live."

According to Rakefet, Zionism means Israel is the home of the Jews. "They can live wherever they want to but Israel will always be their homeland. Israel is like their family. Every Jew is welcome and we live a secular life, not in terms of religion but in terms of people," she said. "The biggest fear of all Jews is that they will have no place to go if they experience persecution. The Holocaust happened seventy years ago and other similar events occurred in Europe and Russia years and years before. The Jews have been persecuted for 2000 years. I can't take the risk that it could happen again. Not for me, not for my children and not for my grandchildren. It is a matter of life and death for me. I will die for that, and it is more than that. I have three sons that will be in the military and could die for their country. Horrible, but that's the way it is."

Rakefet says that Israel is not the safest place in the world to live but it feels safe to her because she is in control of her life and for 2000 years Jews had little control over their lives.

For Rakefet, the security comes from the fact that they have a Jewish prime minister and a Jewish government that works to keep all Jews in the world safe, especially the Jews in Israel. "Jews need to know Israel is their shelter and that whatever happens they have a place to go where they will be safe," she added. "Many say it is a different world and Jews are no longer persecuted, but anti-Semitism does still exists. Not every country is like the United States. For example, there are some places in the world where Jews cannot walk down the street with a yarmulke on their heads and feel safe. There are still many countries like Netherlands, Russia and France where Jews do not feel safe and have to deal with anti-Semitism everyday And to me, it is really ironic, that Israel is where Jews probably pay the highest price for being Jews because of the Palestinian-Israeli conflict."

"Today I think the majority of Israelis are ready for a solution and know that the Gaza Strip and the West Bank won't be part of Israel but will become a Palestinian state or the Palestinian Authority. I think we will eventually be able to set borders with the Palestinians. The Gaza Strip today is Palestinian and does not have any Israeli settlements in it, but it would be impossible to totally evacuate the West Bank so I think about eighty percent of the land will probably go to the Palestinians. The Palestinians want ninety six percent. That leaves sixteen percent to be negotiated."

"The important question, to me, is, 'How are the Palestinians going to manage their lives?' In the Gaza Strip things are not going well. They had democratic elections and Hamas won making the Israelis' fear a reality -- a Palestinian state that is governed by Hamas who is controlled by Iran and who wants to destroy Israel. This situation makes the possibility for a solution in the West Bank even more complicated.

There is no guarantee that the West Bank won't become another Hamas state. So it will be harder to find a solution in the West Bank than it was in Gaza, but we will and I feel certain we eventually will also find a solution for Jerusalem."

"Frankly, I don't think the sixteen percent of the West Bank is the real issue between us; rather it is the willingness of the people in both governments to come to some sort of agreement. The Israeli government went from the political right to almost the political left and holds positions today that twenty years ago were almost unacceptable. Today it is a very balanced government and I believe it is moving toward a solution."

Rakefet says the Palestinians have more power today in Gaza than they ever had, mostly because of Hamas, with its Iranian connections. Iran controls the Palestinians through Hamas and wants to keep things in constant chaos and would rather deal with Israel than have to deal with the United States on nuclear weapons.

She says, "I truly understand the pain of the Palestinians and know that I am responsible for part of this situation and part of their pain. Sometimes there has to be pain and war because we need armies to survive. This is what an army is for -- survival. My fourteen-year old son, who will be in the Israeli army soon, said to me recently that when he was living in Israel he knew he was born a Jew, but living in America he learned that he chooses to be a Jew. He could soon be fighting for his country and I hope he knows what he is fighting for. He is fighting for survival."

Rakefet Gingsberg -West Bank & Resource Issues

Would Israel take down the settlements in the West Bank? Rakefet says, "That is a complicated question and the answer depends on certain circumstances. To have Hamas in the West Bank will cause great fear to the Israelis. Another fear is if there is a Palestinian state, the Palestinians will come into Israel and make claim to former homes and land. This is an issue that Israel has dealt with for years. Israelis realize that the Palestinians will never give up on their land or give up on the right to build their own state. At the same time, Israel is only willing to give consideration to the Gaza Strip and the West Bank as Palestinian territory. That's it."

"The West Bank is complicated and it doesn't look the same as it did forty years ago. There are a lot of Israeli settlements and thousands of Jews living there in big cities. We have checkpoints near the borders and I know that is horrible for the Palestinians, but it is the best way to keep bombs out of our lives and to survive. My supermarket was bombed near Tel Aviv, and that was next to my kid's school. If checkpoints keep that from happening, then we need to do that to survive."

Rakefet says, "I live twenty minutes from Tel Aviv which is the largest city in Israel and I can see the city from my home on the border or Green Line. If we give the Palestinians the West Bank, and Hamas does not vanish -- this will cause great fear that rockets will be sent to Tel Aviv like Gaza keeps sending rockets into other parts of Israel?"

The Palestinians have two main political parties, Hamas and Fatah. Hamas has more power than Fatah does in Gaza and Hamas won the most recent democratic elections. The Palestinians have many social and financial problems and think Hamas is the solution to some of them, but the Palestinians also know that Hamas will not recognize Israel as a state. "That is a problem for me," says Rakefet. "Their government's decisions affect my life, so I care how they manage their lives."

"Eventually we will both have to find a way to make it work. The real problem is that Hamas is controlled by Iran. When the United States deals with Iran, they will find out how complicated it is. Iran makes decisions only for their purposes and these may not even be in the interest of the Palestinians. Their motive is to rid the world of Israel, and they have the money and the power to attempt it. So there is no point in fighting Hamas. The fight is with Iran."

"Emotionally, sometimes I think all this will never end, but I know I need to have hope because there is no alternative. Palestinian and Israelis are talking more at the grass roots level through Restorative Justice programs. Is that going to solve the problems? I don't think so -- the peace process is above us. The Palestinians' problems are mounting and becoming more complicated. They have different groups in their society that are fighting one another. Israel really wants to make peace work. We do try. I think every Israeli would be relieved to see that the Palestinians can manage their lives in a democratic way. If it is a democratic way, it will be better for both sides."

Rakefet concedes that there is a huge water problem in the Mideast that affects many countries.

"It is true that there are aquifers under the West Bank making that situation even more complicated," Rakefet said. Israel is very concerned about losing their water supply. Jordan is out of water and Israel is supplying them with water. It is part of a peace agreement between Jordan and Israel that Jordan gets a certain amount of water even if Israel runs out of water. Strangely enough, the water problem may be what brings peace to us because all the Mideast countries have a severe water problem. We will all have to work together to find a solution to manage the water, that includes Syria, Israel, Jordan, Egypt and Lebanon. Otherwise it is death for everyone."

Epilogue

A Reason to Hope!

It seems clear that Restorative Justice Circles give people a chance to vent their strong emotional feelings in a safe respectful environment. It doesn't matter what type of harm the discussion is about -- international conflict, criminality, or other issues -- the approach is the same.

In a protective setting like a Restorative Justice Circle a person is given permission to let out feelings of frustration or anger that they have toward another and for the other person's ideology -- while at the same time knowing they are going to hear the other side of the story.

Somehow this dynamic set of circumstances seems to help smooth out the tension, because everyone knows they will have a chance to state their side of the issue. Recognition of a common humanity often occurs. Once everyone has had their say, the tension starts to subside and opens up possibilities for reconciliation, no matter how small. Then everyone can look for issues they agree on, move them aside, try to disassemble the issues they can't agree on and work toward solutions.

It is obvious that there are some issues that Rakefet and Othman agree on.

First, it is obvious that they are both deeply emotional about their side of the issue. Also, they agree that when participating in a

Restorative Justice – Healing & Redemption

Restorative Justice Circle, it is better if the participants or their families lived in the country that they represent.

Of the greatest importance, they did, albeit reluctantly for Othman, agree that the Palestinian state would consist of Gaza and the West Bank and that the borders should be secured. They agreed that the status of the city of Jerusalem is a very contentious issue. However, both seemed to hope that some agreement could be reached by recognizing that the three major faiths that are represented there need the members of their specific faith to have access to their holy places. Othman's argument for a multijurisdictional area was interesting. Both, also, concurred that the water situation is dire and will need agreement between all the major Mideast countries to find a resolution.

It seems like the sixteen percent of the West Bank, the refugee issue and the water problem were most divisive. It appears both sides will have to give on the sixteen percent, and because refugees are scattered all over the world, probably most will not return. That, perhaps, could end up solidifying the Palestinian population and eliminate one of the issues.

The water problem appears to be the toughest but at the same time the most necessary and immediate one to resolve. Perhaps as Rakefet said, "It may be, in the end, what really brings peace to the area. Common need may work for the common good otherwise no one wins -- everyone dies."

It is very exciting to note here that a Restorative Justice movement

93

-- working toward peace between the Palestinians and Israelis in their home territory, at a grass-roots level -- began a few years ago. It started when an Israeli father who lost two sons in the conflict was so full of anguish that he felt he had to try to stop the senseless loss of life on both sides. He sought out a Palestinian father who also lost a son and they started a Restorative Justice program called "Hello Shalom!/Hello Salaam!

This is actually a phone line that can be used free of charge for up to thirty minutes anywhere within Israel or the Palestinian territories. It's used to speak with someone on the other side of the conflict who recently lost a loved one and to give them comfort -- or to just speak about peace and reconciliation.

Many callers exchange numbers and maintain contact. Within the first two years of its inception more than 400,000 people participated in over one million phone calls.

This organization has expanded and is part of a greater group called "Parents Circle - Families Forum." There are more than 500 members -- both Israeli and Palestinian -- of this non-profit group who try to promote dialogue and reconciliation. They grieve together and share with one another while breaking down national boundaries. This, in turn, promotes healing -- not revenge. The Parent's Circle believes that Israelis and Palestinians want to, and will, work together for peace. Each member has lost a loved one in the conflict and paid the highest price. This has created an explicit trust between members regardless of what side they are on.

Members of the Parents Circle have had success as a face to face advocacy group for family members on each sides of the conflict, sharing painful personal stories that have great impact. They believe it is impossible to have empathy for one another when one does not understand the culture or personal story of the other. The Parent's Circle spends many hours in classroom dialogues. In 2006 over more than one thousand meetings were held for sixteen and seventeen-year-old Palestinian and Israeli students. This group has many other programs underway. There really is reason to hope!

(Above information was taken Parents Circle - Families Forum website: www.theparentscircle.com)

Section III

Violentization

Why People Become Violent

Restorative Justice empowers victims. As we have seen in the stories of the different victims of crime, they become less frightened, find healing, feel stronger and empowered after they meet face to face with their offenders. Usually, they are surprised to discover that their offender was a victim, too.

In an effort to explain this phenomenon, author Richard Rhodes delves into the work of Dr. Lonnie H. Athens, an American criminologist, in the book "Why They Kill."

Dr. Athens believes, after studying hundreds of violent criminals, their family situations and early development, that people are not born violent but because of their early development they become violent.

He believes there are four stages in this developmental process called violentization and it leaves the person deeply troubled and disturbed. This does not happen overnight but usually happens gradually over a period of time. The four stages are brutalization, belligerency, violent performances and virulency.

The first stage is brutalization where the victim is constantly brutally beaten into submission. Another component of brutalization is personal horrification -- when the victim must watch and listen as a loved one is brutally beaten and they can do nothing to stop it. There is also violent coaching when the victim is told over and over again that the only way to solve interpersonal problems is with violence. The brutalization stage leaves the victim full of rage with a sense of powerlessness. The victim turns his/her feelings inward and feels worthless because of their inability to fight back or to stop the beating of his loved one. The violent coaching just adds to the victim's humiliation and sense of worthlessness.

The important part of the belligerency stage is that the victim suddenly realizes that all the violent coaching applies to him/her -- and that is the answer to victimization. The victim then is convinced that he/she must resort to a violent resolution, defensively, the next time he is seriously challenged.

In the violent performance stage the victim tries out his defensive violent resolution. If he wins a clear victory, people suddenly begin treating him differently -- they start showing him fear and respect. That is a powerful experience and it gives him a new sense of identity as someone who can stand up for himself. Success raises the possibility of moving on to a further state of violence that being *failure.* In the next violent performance he may experience defeat. This often causes him to conclude he needs to avoid physical confrontations and resort to more lethal violence more quickly. Thus, bitter failure at the hand of a foe can have the effect of making the subject more determined than ever to be violent. For the first time he may feel liberated from the violent oppression of others and have a new sense of power.

The virulency stage makes his newly discovered sense of power almost irresistible. The person is no longer a victim and is determined not to tolerate any provocation and to even provoke others. He has suddenly been emboldened and made venomous at the same time by going full circlerom a victim of brutalization to a ruthless aggressor. This move to unmitigated violent resolution completes the last of the four stages of volentization.

Restorative Justice – Healing & Redemption

Violentization is an authentic developmental process and unless someone goes through it, Athens says, he will not become a dangerous violent criminal. Violentization is transmitted expeditiously across generations, Athens observes, as the brutalized evolve into brutalizers, ensuring that there will always be a plentiful supply of new candidates to replace those who lose their lives, are sent to prison or those who undergo maturational reform.

Athens says the transmission is not inevitable. The process from start to finish may take years or run its course in a matter of months. The violent socialization process can be interrupted at any point by effective interventions that divert the person to other alternatives.

When people look at a dangerous violent criminal at the beginning of his developmental process rather than at the very end, they will see, perhaps unexpectedly, that the criminal began as a relatively benign human being for whom they would probably have more sympathy than antipathy. Perhaps more importantly, people will conclude that the creation of dangerous violent criminals is largely preventable, as is much of the human carnage that follows in the wake of their birth. Therefore, if society fails to take significant steps to stop the process behind the creation of dangerous violent criminals, it tacitly becomes an accomplice in creating them.

Richard Rhodes, the author of "Why They Kill" generously gave permission to use the above summarized material from his book.

Rhodes wanted to add and emphasize the following: "Socialization is a process of forming a new identity. We all go through it when we become a doctor or a lawyer, or go through military training, or experience a religious conversion, or recover from a serious accident or the loss of someone we love. Violent socialization is the process of forming a new identity as a violent person."

What I didn't empathize sufficiently in "Why They Kill" is that the violent socialization process can be interrupted at any point along the way by effective interventions that divert the person going through the process to other alternatives. That's where **Restorative Justice** could make a difference -- because violentization is reversible even after someone has gone through to the end, just as any other identity we assume in our lives is reversible.

Note from author of "Restorative Justice Is Changing The World": This could be why we often see the transformation of offenders following face to face dialogue. The Restorative Justice process is so powerful when the offender has to face their victim and makes the decision to become accountable to their victim and community that they choose to drop their identity of violence and choose another path.

"Today's Aggressors are often Yesterday's Victims"
................*Olga Botcharova*

Section IV

Red Hook's Story

Community Models
U. S, Restorative Justice

Brooklyn, N. Y.
Red Hook Community Justice Center

Barron County, WI
Restorative Justice Program

Red Hook
Community Justice Center

How did the Community Justice Center Begin

The Red Hook Community Justice Center in Brooklyn, New York opened its doors in April of 2000 and was the nation's second multi-jurisdictional community court using Restorative Justice practices. The first was opened in midtown Manhattan a few years earlier. Criminal experts, from other states in the United States, and from countries around the world, including England, Wales, Australia and China have visited the community court in midtown Manhattan and the Community Justice Center in Red Hook's with the hope of duplicating similar centers in their own communities.

The Red Hook Community Justice Center began as a result of a tragedy in the community and as a spin-off from the model in midtown Manhattan. At that time, Red Hook contained the second largest public housing complex in the state of New York with eighty-five hundred residents and was the heart of a low-income-minority neighborhood with a total population of eleven thousand. In 1995 a beloved school principal, Patrick Daly, was shot in this crack-infested community while trying to find a truant student. After that, there was a major outcry from the people living in Red Hook that something needed to be done. Everyone said, "If the school principal wasn't safe, no one is safe. Justice needs to come back to our community."

During this same period of time, the Center for Court Innovation, which is the non-profit research arm of the justice system in New York was preparing to start an experiment in community justice. These events converged. District Attorney Charles Hynes, who led the prosecution of the murderers of Patrick Daly and Judith Kaye, Chief Judge of the state of New York along with other criminal justice officials, pinpointed the unsafe, crime-ridden community of Red Hook as the place to start a Community Justice Center. Red Hook would become the most comprehensive court in the state encompassing all three jurisdictions -- criminal, family and civil. They hoped to improve the safety of the neighborhood and enhance the legitimacy of the justice system in the eyes of the local residents by using a five-point approach: promote accountability, repair conditions of disorder, solve underlying problems, engage the community and make justice visible.

Judge Kaye asked Judge Alex Calabrese to be the single judge at the Red Hook Community Justice Center. She knew of his vast experience and his recent innovative work in dealing with substance abuse cases. He was also known for his alignment with many in the Restorative Justice movement who believed in getting as many addicts as possible into treatment. Judge Calabrese accepted the offer and the organizers made sure that he had the funds and all the support he needed on site.

The catchment area (the physical area where Red Hook's criminal cases come from) include three precincts with a population of

210,000 residents. One of those precincts is the Red Hook community which is isolated from the other two precincts by water and an expressway. The Community Justice Center began its operation out of a refurbished Catholic School that was once an important part of the community. Because Judge Calabrese would be the only judge at the center he met with members of Red Hook's low-income, minority community via focus groups. They told him they did not want him to bring a local jail there to lock everybody up. They stated unanimously, "We don't want a jail, we want our people to be given an opportunity, especially our young people because they need all the help they can get. But if they don't take advantage of the help you give them, well, then just throw them in jail and throw away the key." They were tough and they were not kidding -- they were tired of crime. Their focus was on giving positive opportunities to members of the community.

Judge Calabrese asked the focus groups what they wanted to happen with people involved in drug cases and they all said overwhelmingly, **"Get them help."** These people were dads, moms, brothers and sisters of people in Red Hook who understood that the rule is rehabilitation. If someone doesn't accept rehabilitation, the guilty plea is already in place and then you go to jail. So in some ways it is a harsher sentence. Ask any drug addict, "What would you rather do, spend ten days in jail or go to rehab?" most of them will take the ten days in jail. So the community is really being hard on crime. Treatment is very tough. If they make it, they and the community benefit.

Ever since the Justice Center opened, Judge Calabrese has been an incredible inspiration to everyone working there, and they have made great strides in all areas of civil, criminal and family law. The

Judge is particularly enthusiastic about the Center's Drug and Alcohol Court and the success that they are having. Tina, in a previous story, is only one of many success stories.

How Red Hook Functions

The Red Community Justice Center is unique because it recognizes that neighborhood problems do not always conform to the arbitrary jurisdictional boundaries of the modern court system. Because Red Hook is multijurisdictional, the boundaries are flexible and do not inhibit family cases and drug cases to overlap in terms of problem solving. That is one of the secrets of its success.

Anyone arrested in Red Hook is automatically diverted to the Community Justice Center and the case is heard for the first time. All low level felonies, misdemeanors, domestic violence and assault cases come before Judge Calabrese. If it goes beyond that level the case is heard downtown. Most arrests are drug charges, which can be related to weapons charges, shoplifting, prostitution, domestic violence or stealing to support a drug habit. The majority of cases are handled with some sort of alternative program and Restorative Justice processes are offered through a partnering agency called "Safe Horizon." (This is a Community Dispute Resolution Center operating out of an off-site location just minutes away from Red Hook, and services include victim/offender dialogue, mediation, and Restorative Justice circles.)

Most of Red Hook's defendants face a maximum of one year in jail. When a police officer makes an arrest the suspect is held overnight at the precinct and brought before Judge Calabrese in the morning. At that point, the defendant is told what he or she is being charged with and a discussion begins about what alternatives the person can accept. All of this happens within twenty-four hours.

Drug Cases at Red Hook

The overall community problem in Red Hook is drugs. The Community Justice Center is unique in many ways and has one of the most successful and innovative programs in how substance abuse, namely drugs and alcohol problems, are handled.

People on drugs lie, cheat and steal and manipulate the people around them plus the different situations they are in to continue to use drugs. The programs offered at the Red Hook Community Justice Center are making a difference by approaching the drug problem from a more humane and practical angle.

Every Thursday is set aside to hear substance-abuse cases. People who are referred to the court that day are put on a list that gives their current and past criminal information which includes what they are presently charged with and if they are in treatment. In fact, every person, charged at Red Hook is put into a very extensive database and all relevant information on each individual can be accessed by the Judge, the defense attorney and prosecutor plus other service providers in the community center at any time.

Red Hook's Project Director, James Brodick says, "Instead of jail sentences, the drug court has different sanctions that can be imposed like treatment-ready programs, which are really drug education classes that can be mandated three times a week or five times a week. Depending on the case, the addict can go from outpatient to attentive out-patient (closer supervision). Also, they can go from outpatient to residential if necessary or go to long-term residential.

There are several different court responses. The Judge likes to hear recommendations from the on-site clinic, 'Therapeutically what does this person need?'"

"With substance abuse there is usually a lapse along the way. It is very rare that somebody comes in and the court says, 'Do this or else,' and they go into treatment and are clean the whole time. So the reality is that we have to be understanding to the therapeutic process, and that's the balance and the challenge that we face here every day."

Brodick adds, "Judge Calabrese understands this therapeutic approach as well as anybody and understands that relapse is part of recovery and so does the district attorney's office. Sometimes the process requires that the Judge needs to give a sanction, a stern talk, maybe give a couple days of community service on top of what they are already doing or he asks them to write an essay about how their substance abuse is affecting their family. This is very effective, because the judge will use that essay to refer to later and remind the addict of their family. This gives the Judge the opportunity to personalize the situation and what was written in the essay can even be used as leverage. There is a lot of dialogue between the judge and the defendant which you normally would not see in a court setting.

If someone needs counseling or family mediation the Judge can mandate that. There is supervised community service work for the drug addicts to do. This includes painting over graffiti, gardening projects, working in the parks etc. Their community service starts immediately after they see the Judge. If they don't do what they are supposed to do, then a warrant goes out for their arrest. If they need child care while doing their community service commitment, that's available to them at the center and it's free.

When there are on-site services there are fewer people going to jail, which actually saves money for the taxpayer's, because in the end, treatment is cheaper than jail, and certainly has better long-term potential.

Drug Courts are included in Restorative Justice Practices and started in this country in the 1990s. The main criticism of them was that they were soft on crime. However, when dealing with non-violent crimes, related to addiction, it soon became evident that these people needed treatment and this gave many back their lives and enabled them to become contributing members of society.

Retention not Recidivism

In the drug treatment world the challenge is retention. If you ask a police officer, "What is most frustrating about your job?" He or she will say, "Rearresting the same person over and over again."

Brodick said, "What we learned about having people in drug-treatment programs is that somebody who has been treated for even six months may have a lapse. Even if they don't complete the program and the judge has to put them in jail their number of arrests during that time often drops significantly and sometimes the person does not get rearrested.

So we are trying to track retention rates and completion rates. We have an on-site evaluator that keeps track of why some programs are more successful than others. African-American women are failing in drug treatment at higher rates than any other group of people and we are trying to find out why. When people do complete drug treatment we know that they are forty percent less likely to get rearrested within a year's time than someone who hasn't. At Red Hook there are usually about one hundred and twenty people and about twenty-five juveniles in treatment at one point in time."

Judge Calabrese states, I don't give sanctions unless I have to, which means that the addict may get arrested again. They are using drugs. Is that a failure? No. The person needs to stop the drugs. Trial and error are acceptable. Sometimes they are arrested three times before I put them in residential treatment for a year because I need the leverage of a jail sentence for repeated offenses. I don't have the leverage on the first arrest to do what really needs to be done therapeutically, unless it is voluntary. They can graduate from the program in 18 months. The measurement is retention. Recidivism is not a good measurement for drugs and alcohol."

"After someone finishes drug treatment, I congratulate them and I try to line them up with job training and go forward. When we opened the Red Hook Community Justice Center we were surprised, actually almost shocked, that we were able to get so much treatment and services for these low-levels crimes. We are able to do this because we have social workers on-site to do evaluations and we create linkage with other programs. Also, I have an agreement with the lawyers who come before me that if we put people in treatment and they fail, they need to be understanding. Addicts often need to be given a number of reasonable opportunities to do what they need to do."

Judge Calabrese adds, "The defense attorneys need to recognize that this is a process -- when their clients have been given every reasonable opportunity to do what they need to do the reward at the end is sometimes that the district attorney will dismiss the case. Sometimes it isn't. But our focus is to help their clients and we're not setting them up to fail. That is an important step because we don't get any of these individuals in treatment unless the defense lawyer says we can talk to their client. When we can talk to the defendant the lawyer then discusses what we say with his client. The defendant will often actually ask to do treatment because it is always presented as an option in their case."

"Too many prosecutors are all about winning trials and putting people in jail, and for defense attorneys it is about getting the person off. But at Red Hook things operate differently. We work toward co-operation between myself and the attorneys for the benefit of the individual. The other day I heard a prosecutor at Red Hook say, 'What is great about being a prosecutor at Red Hook is that you really can try and do justice by looking at each case individually.'"

Judge Calabrese continues, "Over time we have developed trust with the defense attorneys, the district attorney, the court personnel and the police officers working in the community. If they see a drug addict on the street corner the day after he was arrested, they know there is a good likelihood that person will eventually get the treatment they need. We did not just give them a slap on the wrist, but we care, and the officers understand our procedures and therapeutic process. The alternative is jail. Communicating is important so we give the officers feedback from the court. That's teamwork. You can't have that on a large scale -- you need a smaller community to work in. Drugs are like a fungus and very difficult to deal with as far as the impact on the justice system and the community."

Red Hook offers Role Models

"Many generations live in Red Hook but in the past there has been a lack of role models," says Judge Calabrese. "People who are successful usually move out. The great thing about our youth programs is that we do a great job of role modeling for these kids. The court officers talk to them, the lawyers talk to them, and a lot of youth counselors are also talking to them. There are constant opportunities for interaction with Red Hook's young people at the Community Justice Center and the youth court. If you talked to our teenagers who were members of the youth court a few years ago, they would not have been going to college. But now when you talk to them, they are all talking about getting into college. They have future plans and future goals. They get that from all the role modeling here at Red Hook. These kids can be just as successful as anyone else. Tremendous differences have occurred since we opened in 2000 and it emphasizes how we can help the community. We target our programs to focus on the 11,000 people that live in one square mile. People who live in a one million dollar brownstone do not need us but these people do."

James Brodick, the Project Director at Red Hook grew up in the Red Hook Community and could not be a better role model for the community. He is a highly capable young man, very proud of his accomplishments and equally proud of the transformation of his hometown.

Many who work at the Justice Center also make a huge effort to focus on the community with programs outside of the court room.

Restorative Justice – Healing & Redemption

One of the ways, is supporting a baseball program in which one hundred and fifty kids participate and getting businesses to sponsor teams so the kids can play for free. People from the community and the courthouse volunteer to help out. Last year they had over one hundred volunteers.

The Red Hook story goes far beyond what happens in the courtroom because the Center is the hub for an array of unconventional programs that engage local residents in "doing justice." These include mediation, community service projects that put local volunteers to work repairing conditions of disorder and a youth court where teenagers resolve actual cases involving their peers. The idea here is to engage the community in aggressive crime prevention, solving local problems before they even come to court. The Community Justice Center is very accessible to the community and relationships have developed with community members and court personnel, prosecutors, defense attorneys and police officers. After a period of time of working together, they have learned to trust one another and work toward the improvement of their community.

Red Hook has "Proven" its Success!

Judge Calabrese accesses Restorative Justice processes through a partnering agency called "Safe Horizon" that operates in an off-site location just minutes away from Red Hook. The Restorative Justice facilitators from "Safe Horizon" were trained by Dr. Umbreit. The Judge also has sixteen on-site partnering agencies with an array of sanctions and services at his immediate disposal including community restitution projects, educational workshops, job development, a clinic with social workers and case managers, GED classes, medical care, drug treatment and mental health counselling rigorously monitored to ensure accountability and individual responsibility. Plus they now have a computer center with a full-time teacher five days a week. This center is funded by a local business and it provides programing to help people get jobs. The goal is to offer a coordinated approach to problems in Red Hook's neighborhood that include issues like drugs, crime, domestic violence and landlord-tenant disputes.

Brodick said, "We also put emphasis on prevention, which is a key component to our success. Included are a whole array of youth programs, an HIV and substance abuse program, a youth court and a summer internship program for kids."

"New York's Center for Court Innovation and Court Administration listened to the people of Red Hook, when they said a criminal court case affects the rest of a person's life," said Judge Calabrese. "For example, they said, if a person takes a guilty plea on a drug case and even if they go into treatment and that person does everything they are supposed to do, that guilty plea could get them thrown out of their public housing. Downtown a criminal court judge does not pay attention to those things. Their basic thought is, 'You want to take a guilty plea then you have to go into treatment.' The case is resolved. They don't know about the rest of their life and quite frankly they don't care. Here, at Red Hook, we do care and somebody is there asking the questions. So when we see a public housing address we try to work with the defense attorney and prosecutor to see how we can get this person in treatment so that they don't lose their home. Because you get somebody cleaned up and off drugs and they have no shelter when they get released, what's the point."

"By the same token, if a single mom gets arrested on a drug charge she has the potential of losing her home as well as her children. So we try to be very careful how we get people services to help them but not separate families. Really, what we are doing here is recognizing what a court case can do to the rest of your life. Sometimes a court case causes additional harm even when you are trying to use problem solving. That is why we are a multijurisdictional court because we can deal with many different issues concerning families in one court with one judge. Usually courts handle matters that are heard by different decision makers at different locations.

Judge Calabrese is the only judge and the biggest decision maker at Red Hook. Everyone agrees, he is a major part of Red Hook's proven success because of his inspirational, compassionate leadership and his intense devotion to what he believes is the only answer to our nation's crime problems: Restorative Community Justice. The Judge says, "I was lucky enough to be noticed by Judge Kaye and given an opportunity to come to Red Hook and be the only Judge for the Community Justice Center." He added, "I signed up and feel lucky to be here."

In 2008, Red Hook has numerous measures that can prove they have been tremendously successful. People still go to jail, people still lose their apartment and children are remanded. The difference is that the Justice Center is very aware of what is happening in the community around them and are closely connected to its people. They are closing the gaps in the justice system.

Brodick says, "We track a lot of different measurements concerning our court's success and compare ourselves to downtown courts. Our compliance rate throughout our social services and community service is around eighty percent. City wide it is fifty percent. What we are saying is that we are much more successful at getting individuals to start and finish programs.

"Also, if members of the community feel physically safe, it is measurable; because once you can established that a community is safe you get merchants coming in bringing jobs. As a consequence, the area becomes prosperous. That is now occurring in Red Hook. We are not the total reason for this positive change but we are an important part. People will go out shopping if they feel safe, go to restaurants, go to movies, etc. If you can look down the road, change a neighborhood and get people safe, you get merchants investing in your community and it can make all the difference. You need to change the public perception both literally and actually and you will get results."

The Red Hook Community Justice Center is the product of a unique public-private partnership that has engaged all levels of government -- city, county, state and federal. Planning was led by the Center for Court Innovation and funding is provided by the New York State Unified Court System and the City of New York. A variety of government and private funds also provide ongoing support. The Justice Center's model of public-private partnership extends beyond funding -- it relies on an array of institutional partners to identify local problems, supervise community service and offer on-site social services.

Congratulations to the state of New York, Chief Judge Judith Kaye, Judge Alex Calabrese, Project Director James Brodick and all the wonderful people working at Red Hook. The have all put their hearts and souls into helping the community turn into a prosperous safe place to live, where you can find jobs and raise a family. Red Hook is a model for the nation and the world!

Models of Restorative Justice Programs

Restorative Justice Programs are best designed to fit the needs of an individual community, small or large in population.

In an effort to assist communities that are trying to put together a Restorative Justice program for their community two examples follow as models for implementation.

The first one is the Red Hook Community Justice Center in Brooklyn, New York, a larger community; and the second is Barron County, Wisconsin, a smaller community.

The two necessary components -- no matter what the size of the community -- is an Inspirational Leader and Funding!

Organizational Chart

Red Hook Community Justice Center Brooklyn, New York

Project Director

Deputy Directory
Research - Research Associate
Mentoring & Internships - Director of Youth Programs
Director of Programs - Coordinator of Americorps & Youth Court
Youth Echo - Manager & Community Outreach Coordinator
(Program for teens who want to speak out about
issues that concern them) Use Partner Agencies

Project Director

Criminal Court
Clinic Director - Senior Case Manager - Social Worker
Partner Agency - **Safe Horizon** assists with processes of
Restorative Justice victim/offender dialogue & mediation, etc.
Coordinator of Alternative Sanctions - Intake Specialist

Family Court
Clinical Director - Coordinator of Youth/Family Services
Use of Partner Agencies
Housing/ Mediation - Housing Resource Coordinator
Office/Facilities - Facility Manager - Supervisors - Custodian

Red Hook
Commuity Justice Center's
Community Services

A project of the New York State Unified Court System, the Red Hook Community Justice Center is the nation's first multi-jurisdictional community court and houses a range of services available to all community residents on a walk-in basis. All services are free and confidential.

Free Child Care - The Justice Center offers free child care in a secure area designated for children and is available for everyone who makes use of services, appears in court or needs to do community service.

Mediation - Mediation can be used to settle youth, family, housing and neighborhood disputes. These services are available for all community residents.

Drug Treatment - In partnership with other providers, Phoenix House provides a short-term treatment readiness program and referrals to long term treatment for young people and adults.

Housing Court Resource Center - Free legal information and referrals are available to landlords and tenants with housing issues, including court cases, code compliance and rental assistance.

Health Services - Community Health Care Network provides basic health service to persons involved with the court and walk-ins.

Domestic Violence Support Group - Safe Horizon provides a domestic violence counselor to assist in the procurement of orders of protection, make referrals to community-based services and addresses other issues related to domestic violence. Also, they handle Restorative Justice processes for Red Hook.

Mental Health - Clinic staff is the link to counseling and other mental health services for adult and juvenile clients, for family members and for all local residents.

Youth and Family Services - A Good Shepherd Services Social Worker is on-site to provide crisis intervention, clinical/mental health assessments, and referrals to neighborhood-based services for youth and families.

Adult Education - The Justice Center hosts GED classes run by the Department of Education. Off-site education services are available to people ages 17-20.

Job Placement - Resume writing and job development services are available to litigants and walk-ins through a job developer employed by an outside agency.

Red Hook Youth Court - The Youth Court trains youth to serve as judge, jury and attorney, hearing real cases of members of their peer group (ages 10 to 17) who admit responsibility for low-level offenses such as truancy and disorderly conduct. In the process, the Youth Court works to develop youth into leaders of their community and engage them in positive activities. The members of the Youth Court meet twice weekly and earn a monthly stipend.

Mentoring and Internships - The Red Hook Youth Court sponsors summer internships with agencies in Red Hook and other parts of New York City and coordinates a mentoring program that matches local young people with caring, responsible adults.

Red Hook Public Safety Corps - Every year, 50 residents commit to a year of community service, such as fixing locks, aiding victims, tutoring children. In return, Corps members receive job training, a living stipend, free child care and an educational grant.

TEACH - Twice a year, twenty teens are chosen to take part in a three-month training course to become peer educators for the prevention of HIV and substance abuse. They then conduct two-hour workshops for other teens in Brooklyn. The peer educators meet twice weekly and earn a monthly stipend.

Community Initiatives - The Justice Center organizers assist neighborhood residents in developing creative and lasting solutions to community problems. They have worked on a variety of community initiatives, including illegal dumping and the revitalization of a nearby park.

Organizational Chart

Barron County's
Restorative Justice Program

This model represents the very successful Restorative Justice program that was put into action in the year 2000 in Barron County, Wisconsin. The Founder was the Honorable Edward R. Brunner, who at the time, was the Circuit Court Judge of Barron County. He envisioned Restorative Justice making a real difference in his community and played a major supportive role.

Polly Wolner became the Executive Director of Barron County's Restorative Justice Program and has been a passionate leader and is responsible, in many ways, for its incredible success. She says, "Judge Brunner was brilliant because he had a hands-off approach and gave the program to the community from the beginning."

(Much of the following information was taken from Barron County's website: www.bcrjp.org)

Restorative Justice – Healing & Redemption

Organization, Job Descriptions and Programs

Founder

Executive Director

Board of Directors
Directors at Large

Staff

Executive Director
Office Manager
Director of Victim Offender Conferencing, Teen Court & Program Coordinator
30 Trained Volunteer Facilitators
Director Restorative Action Program
Outreach Team (3 members)

Crime Prevention Programs

Prime for Life Program
Victim Impact Panel
Self-Study YES (Youth Educational Shoplifting)
Parent-Teen Workshop

Restorative Justice – Healing & Redemption

Job Descriptions

Founder - Leader in the Community in Criminal Justice - Judge/DA/ Chief of Police

Board of Directors - Executive Director-Polly Wolner - The executive committee consists of: President (Superintendent of Schools); Vice President (Professor from the University of Wisconsin); Treasurer (Sheriff) & Secretary (Director of Barron County Health & Human Services).

Directors at Large - Attorney and Municipal Judge, Barron County Board Supervisors, Barron County Circuit Court Judge, Minister - Presbyterian Church, Dean - University of Wisconsin at Barron County, Principal - Elementary School, Guidance Counselor - Barron County Schools, Police Officer - School Liaison, Business Consultant - Self-employed, Corrections Field Supervisor - Dept. of Corrections, COO of Programs and Services - Goodwill Industries.

Executive Director - Follow directives from the Board. Oversee all paid personnel and volunteers working for the Barron County Justice Program, Inc. Raises funds for salaries and programs offered. (paid employee)

Office Manager - Manage all personnel matters and administration of all programs offered. Keep an accurate file system of cases handled by BCRJ and statistics on those cases. Grant reporting and all clerical and filing associated with BCRJ. (paid employee)

Director of Victim/Offender Conferencing, Teen Court & Program Coordinator - Oversees and trains 30 plus volunteer facilitators used in Victim/Offender Conferencing. Director of Teen Court and coordinates programs for prevention of criminal behavior. (paid employee)

Restorative Justice – Healing & Redemption

Victim Offender Conferencing is at the heart of the Restorative Justice system. The director oversees a process that provides interested victims of crime the opportunity to meet their offenders in a safe and structured setting, with the goal of holding the offenders directly accountable for their behavior while providing important assistance and compensation to the victims. With the assistance of a trained facilitator, the victims are able to let the offenders know how the crimes affected them, receive answers to their questions, and to be directly involved in developing a restitution plan for the offenders. The offenders are able to take direct responsibility for their behavior, to learn the full effect of what they did, and develop a plan for making things right with the person(s) they violated.

The Director also oversees a Restorative Justice Teen Court that helps juvenile offenders restore their relationships with the community through alternative methods of adjudicating minor juvenile offenses, including programs that teach responsibility and positive decision making and restore a sense of safety in the community.

Outreach Team (3 Members) Preventive Program

Barron County Restorative Justice Programs, Inc. in partnership with the school districts in their county and the Barron County Department of Health and Human Services has hired and trained three community outreach workers to work in these school districts. Their job is to identify and intervene in pre-truancy and truancy issues with students and implement appropriate restorative interventions to resolve the attendance issues and the underlying issues contributing to the attendance problem.

Restorative Action Program - The RAP program consists of education and community service as a structure to teach the offender that behavior does matter and does affect the community. This allows the young offender to provide a service to their community in lieu of a citation.

Restorative Justice – Healing & Redemption

Crime Prevention Programs

Victim Impact Panel - These panels consist of a small group of victims of drunk driving tragedies or property crimes who relate how their lives have been affected by the sudden loss of a loved one or the violation of a crime committed against them. Sometimes the panel also includes offenders, not with the purpose to blame or judge them, but to affect the audience on an emotional level by telling their stories. Victim impact panels are designed to change the behavior of offenders. Listening to personal accounts of drunk driving tragedies or property crime helps offenders realize the dangers and consequences of their behavior. At the same time, victim impact panels can be very helpful in the healing process of panel participants.

In Barron County, not only offenders attend victim impact panels but anyone who attends driver's ed classes is required to attend a victim impact panel of drunk drivers and their victims' family and friends.

Prime for Life - This twelve-hour course is offered for juveniles who violate drinking laws, school policy, drinking and driving laws, or simply make high-risk choices. It is designed to reduce the risk for problems and focus on three measurable behavioral prevention goals: increase abstinence for a lifetime; delay the age of first use of alcohol; and reduce high-risk choices. The intervention goals include: facilitate self assessment of drinking and drug choices; reduce high-risk use among people who do not already have alcoholism or other drug addiction; facilitate entry into evaluation to determine whether alcoholism or other drug addictions are present; facilitate entry into some form of treatment or a self-help group for those who have already developed alcoholism or other drug addiction; and support abstinence for all people with alcoholism and other drug addiction. Attendees must pay forty dollars for this program.

Restorative Justice – Healing & Redemption

Parent-Teen Workshop - As a consequence of having to appear in Teen Court the teenagers and their parents are required to attend a parent-teen workshop. The cost is $60 and is required. The workshop is staffed by a professionally trained person.

Self-Study YES Program (YES - Youth Educational Shoplifting) - As a sanction for our Teen Court program as well as direct referrals from law enforcement and municipal courts, the YES program for juvenile shop-lifters is offered. The course consists of 5-6 hours of "offense-specific" education with audio CD's and a workbook that the juvenile may keep after completion of the program. The educational topics include, how shoplifting affects the lives of real people (not just stores), the law and its consequences, security technology used in stores, how much they risk for a small reward, how their personal and social pressures can trigger a shoplifting incident, that shoplifting can become addictive, and how to stop shoplifting now and for the rest of their lives. Recidivism rates are reported between 1.3% and 2.7% nationally. The juveniles give the YES Program an average grade of 95% regarding its usefulness to them.

Barron County funds their Restorative Justice Program with funds from the following areas: Federal funds, county funds, grants, paid programs they offer and from training given by the staff to other communities. They house their offices in the Goodwill facility in their community and operate as a non-profit.

Their success with juvenile offenders is documented. The Restorative Justice Program was instituted half-way through the year 2000. The caseload began to steadily drop and in 2005 the average arrest rate for juveniles declined forty five percent in Barron County compared to the state's nineteen percent. Amazing!

Restorative Justice – Healing & Redemption

Thank Yous & Appreciation

to the victims, survivors and offenders who had the courage to tell
their true personal Restorative Justice Stories for this book!!

Maggie & Bill

Kathy & Todd

JJ

Tina

To the following people who contributed personal stories of
their experience with Restorative Justice!!

Allan MacCae

Othman Atta

Rakefet Ginsberg

Acknowledgements

Brooklyn, New York
Judge Alex Calabrese & James Brodick, Project Director
Red Hook Community Justice Center

Minneapolis, Minnesota
Dr. Mark Umbreit, Director Center for Restorative Justice & Peacemaking

Trenton, New Jersey
Gary Hilton, Assistant Commissioner, Department of Corrections, New Jersey
Warden of New Jersey's Maximum-Security Prison

Harrisonburg, Virginia
Dr. Howard Zehr, Professor - Center for Justice & Peacemaking
Eastern Mennonite University - Author of many books on Restorative Justice

Wisconsin
Judge Edward R. Brunner - Appellate Judge, Wausau
Professor Janine Geske - Restorative Justice - Marquette Law School
Pete DeWind, Univ. of Wisconsin, Madison - Law School - Dir. Remington Center
Othman Atta, Attorney at Law - Milwaukee
Rakefet Gingsberg - American Jewish Federation - Milwaukee
Assistant District Attorney - David Lerman - Milwaukee
Barron County - *Polly Wolner - Executive Director, Restorative Justice*
Dane County - *Joe Moser, Colleen Jo Winston, Sherri Gatts*
Dodge County - *Judge Andrew Bissonnette*
Jefferson County - *Judge Jackie Erwin, Tom Schleitwiler*
Washington County - *Mike Bloedorn*

New Zealand
Allan MacRae, Youth Justice Practice Advisor - Southern New Zealand

Restorative Justice – Healing & Redemption

References

"Changing Lenses" by Howard Zehr

"Circle Processes" by Kay Pranis

"Critical Issues in Restorative Justice" by Howard Zehr & Barb Toews

"Deathquest II" by Robert M. Bohm

"Good Courts" by Greg Berman & John Feinblatt

"Guide for Implementing the Comprehensive Strategy for Serious, Violent and Chronic Juvenile Offenders" - U.S. Department of Justice

"Implementing the Balanced and Restorative Justice Model"
U. S. Department of Justice

"Just & Painful" by Graeme Newman

"Marquette Law Review", Vol. 89, Winter 2005, No. 2

"Restorative Justice" by Howard Zehr

"The Courage to Heal" by Ellen Bass and Laura Davis

"The Cure of Troy," a version of Sophocles' Philoctetes by Seamus Heaney

"The Handbook of Restorative Justice - A Global Perspective" by Dr. Sullivan

"The Little Book of Family Group Conferences" by Allan MacRae & Howard Zehr

"The Little Book of Restorative Justice" by Howard Zehr

"The Little Book of Trauma Healing" by Carolyn Yoder

"Theories of Crime" by Daniel J. Curran & Claire M. Renzetti

"Transcending" by Howard Zehr

"Why They Kill" by Richard Rhodes